A Journal of the Seasons

A Journal
of the Seasons
on an Ozark Farm

Leonard Hall

Illustrations by George Conrey

University of Missouri Press
Columbia & London
1980

Copyright © 1980 by
The Curators of the University of Missouri
University of Missouri Press, Columbia, Missouri 65211
Library of Congress Catalog Card Number 80-17831
Printed and bound in the United States of America

Library of Congress Cataloging in Publication Data

Hall, Leonard, 1899-
    A Journal of the Seasons on an Ozark Farm.

    Originally published under title: Country year.
    1. Farm life—Missouri—Caledonia. 2. Caledonia,
Mo. Possum Trot Farm. 3. Natural history—Missouri—
Caledonia. 4. Seasons—Missouri—Caledonia. 5. Hall,
Leonard, 1899-   I. Title.
S521.5.M8H34 1980   977.8'64'043   80-17831
ISBN 0-8262-0317-5
ISBN 0-8262-0326-4 (cloth edition)

To Virginia | *Comrade in the good adventure*

preface to new edition

Each quarter century brings changes in American life, and nowhere is this more true than in farming. Thus it seemed sensible to read again our brief preface to *Country Year* to see whether the same words would apply after thirty-five years at Possum Trot Farm. As stated then, our book is in no sense a treatise on agriculture. Yet it does represent two ordinary people experiencing a new way of life and finding it good.

The years have brought no change in this conclusion. But we began here and spent our first twenty-five years as working farmers, improving our land and raising good beef cattle. Now time has brought far-reaching changes in agriculture—and starting out today on a course similar to ours would necessitate weighing an entirely different set of conditions and values. Yet even doing this, we feel we would somehow make much the same choice as we did thirty-five years ago.

We came to this Ozark valley at a critical moment in American history and American agriculture. A major war had just ended, a war that had put pressures on many areas of farming. It was, moreover, a time of tremendous technological change plus a time when not only America but also much of the world was experiencing a population explosion.

One thing clear was that many American farmers after the war were facing a crisis, resulting in large measure from unsound land use. War and the growing demand for food had resulted over a long period of years in heavy cropping of the semiarid lands of our "near-west" that we call the wheat belt. This plus a long series of dry years had brought on the era of the dust bowl. A similar condition held for the range lands farther west that had been sadly depleted by overgrazing. In the "cotton south" the great problem was erosion, with gullies in once-productive lands deep enough to hide whole farmsteads. Even in the highly productive croplands of the Middle West, monoculture and the failure to build organic matter and high fertility through crop rotation and the plowing down of green manure crops were causing trouble.

The first real American soil conservation movement was born during those years and served as the basis for our own farm program. To the West, shelter belts of trees were planted to check the winds that lifted soil. Thousands of plowed acres were returned to the grass that was their native cover. In the South, diversified farming and crop rotation checked the soil loss. The productive lands of the Middle West were terraced and we built sodded waterways to handle the runoff. We dug thousands of farm ponds for livestock water and planted thousands of new fence rows. Diversification and crop rotation became the order of the day and soil fertility started to climb again.

Here at Possum Trot we worked to help build the organization called Friends of the Land, whose purpose was to create better understanding between city and country people. Through this membership we came to know and work with many of the nation's top conservationists. There was Hugh Bennett (Big Hugh), who founded and directed the nationwide Soil Conservation Service. Chester C. Davis, former president of the St. Louis Federal Reserve Bank, was a talented business executive who showed how to back the conservation movement with adequate financing. Leaders at the University of Missouri were ecologist Rudolf Bennitt and world-famous soil scientist William Albrecht.

Along with soil conservation came a new interest in wildlife. Here in Missouri we built the finest Conservation

Department in the nation by removing wildlife and resource management from politics. On the national scene we came to know Aldo Leopold of Wisconsin whose book *A Sand County Almanac* became the foundation for a new land ethic. And there were Syd Stephens of our Conservation Commission, Lyle Watts of the Forest Service, and many more.

One conservation leader of that era was *not* a university-trained scientist, but a novelist turned farmer. This was Louis Bromfield of Malabar Farm in Ohio, a delightful fellow who managed his land well, was active in every conservation organization, and yet kept on writing. A half dozen of his books grace our shelves today, with autographs that make us proud of our small part in the conservation movement.

It is not surprising that these interests took us into writing—a column that ran for thirty-two years in the two St. Louis dailies and dozens of magazine articles. The column came to the attention of leading conservation organizations, and soon we were lecturing and serving on the boards of the Humane Society of the United States, Defenders of Wildlife, The Nature Conservancy, and the National Parks Association on whose board we remained as a trustee for twenty-five years. Somewhere along the way we acquired a 16 mm. movie camera and were soon photographing wildlife in its wilderness background. Thereafter for a dozen years we lectured and showed our films across the United States, Canada, and the Caribbean for the National Audubon Society

Nor was our outdoor recreational life neglected during those years, despite the farming. Our canoe knew all the rivers of the Ozarks and resulted in the highly successful book *Stars Upstream*. We packed on horseback into the high Cascades, saw the beautiful Dall sheep and moose of the Yukon, photographed the bird life of the Everglades, and even managed a half dozen sorties into the lands of our Latin neighbors to the South.

Through all the years we watched the steady change that was overtaking American agriculture. Farms grew steadily larger and farm families in hundreds of thousands were forced from the land. Technology changed the methods we knew. The machinery grew bigger, season after season. The twelve-plow tractor and giant harvesting combine no longer fitted the hundred acre farm. Fields were thrown together, fence rows were cleared away, terraced lands were leveled.

During these decades our agriculture has returned again to monoculture. Single crops on huge acreages year after year become the order of the day. Yields are boosted by applying chemical fertilizers. Crops are cultivated with chemical herbicides and sprayed with chemical pesticides. Farm-made manure and crop rotation became almost a thing of the past. Cattle, hogs, and poultry are raised in confinement. Steers in hundreds of thousands are fattened in giant feed lots; sows farrow on metal-slatted floors in huge farrowing houses; broilers and laying hens by millions spend their short lives crowded into wire-floored poultry tenements.

Each year we watch three million acres of prime cropland disappear beneath the asphalt parking area of the shopping center or into lots to house our burgeoning population. We see energy costs in agriculture climb until they sometimes exceed the energy produced by the crop being raised. We learn that soil erosion today exceeds what it was before we discovered how to control it. We see our precious soil ingredients shipped off to feed the hungry throughout the world—yet already we search abroad for new sources for these very ingredients.

Whether all this makes for a happier, richer life for tomorrow is hard to say. Our own belief, formed by our years on the land, is that if man is to survive, he must develop what Leopold called "a new land ethic." He must learn that land is not a commodity to be bought, used, worn out, and thrown away, but a precious resource to be cared for, renewed by a constant return of the elements we take away. Only thus can we produce true conservation—the thing that Leopold called "a state of harmony between man and the land."

Thus we must end our preface with the very words that Leopold used to conclude *A Sand County Almanac,* some forty years ago, when he said: "We are remodeling the Alhambra with a steam shovel, and we are proud of our yardage. We shall hardly relinquish the shovel, which after all has many good points. But we are in need of gentler and more objective criteria for its successful use."

L. H.
Caledonia, Missouri
June 1980

contents

Foreword *by Chester C. Davis*   ix

Preface   xiii

SPRING

MARCH   3

A Million Stars – Wild Geese – No Other Life – The Lost
Calf – Making Beef – Country Adventures – Brisk Bidding

APRIL   27

Wondrous Awakening – Time of Singing – Woodcock –
Wildlife Tribulations

MAY   37

Lushness After Rain – Lessons in Nature – Farming Curi-
osities – Fishing on a May Evening – Lively Adventures –
Living with the Country

SUMMER

JUNE   59

Ripening Grain – Eyes That Cannot See – All Nature
Sings – Migrating with Man – Time to Think – Magic
Hour

JULY 78

Drought – Hound Music – Bursts of Blooms – Old Swimming Hole – Fishing at Sunrise

AUGUST 94

The Pond – Country Sounds – Mowing Clover – Feeders

AUTUMN

SEPTEMBER 113

Nothing Really Dies – Storekeeper – Living Off the Country – A Helping Hand for Bees

OCTOBER 124

Blue Shadows Across the Hills – The Groundhog – Insects' Last Stand – Shore Birds Head South

NOVEMBER 137

Late Autumn Days – Country Station – Time for Reflection – First Quail Hunt – Deer Crossing

WINTER

DECEMBER 159

Winter Hills – Butchering Day – Ice Storm – City Cow – Country Christmas – Early Snow

JANUARY 181

A New Year Begins – Myriads of Months – "Nature Stuff" – The Sun Starts North – Big Farms or Small

FEBRUARY 195

Zero Weather – Wildlife in Winter – Philosophy of the Fields – Animals at Play – Spring Edges Closer

foreword

by

CHESTER C. DAVIS

Former President, Federal Reserve Bank of St. Louis

This book will bring life very close to you as the seasons of the year wheel their full cycle on and around Possum Trot Farm in the eastern Missouri Ozarks. Living the *Country Year* through with the Halls will be a warming, fascinating experience. I turned the last page of the manuscript with sadness that there was no more.

Leonard Hall is a mid-Twentieth Century Thoreau. Unlike Thoreau, with him love of the land comes first; his social and economic philosophy as it emerges derives from that. There is nothing ponderous or pontifical in his writing. It is direct and clear as befits the surroundings in which he works and writes. When his musings lead him to express opinion about farm policy, or man's relation to the land, he doesn't labor the point but gives it to you short and sharp. It comes on you like a pepper-ball in a mouthful of the country sausage he temptingly describes.

Fifteen years ago Len and Ginnie Hall set out to prove that it is possible to work in a great city and still enjoy the advantages of real country living. After five years they felt they had the answer. While he was doing well in a highly competitive business in St. Louis, he and his wife had developed the first Possum Trot Farm, their "house in the woods" a few miles south of the city. It was happy proof that man can make a living in town, live close to nature in the country, and thereby find peace.

Meanwhile the occasional article on events and observations at Possum Trot and afield written for the *St. Louis Post Dispatch* grew into a regular column, an outstanding feature of that great metropolitan daily. More and ever more people found their way to the little house under the persimmon tree. The avocation was on its way to become a vocation. Then, ten years ago, they replaced the small "city man's farm" with a farm close by the scenes of his boyhood among old friends in the beautiful Ozark valley called Bellevue, some ninety miles southwest of St. Louis.

This Possum Trot is a real farm, 200 acres of rolling land snuggling up to Buford Mountain which you will grow to know as you go along with the story. Len Hall's return here "belonged to be," as the Ozark saying goes. It was fore-shadowed nearly forty years earlier, in his youthful conviction that, though his family lived in St. Louis, he himself belonged out in the country with Grandpa Hall where he spent summers and every possible weekend. The move was not a shift but a broadening and deepening in the purpose of the adventure in living on which the Halls had embarked five years before. They would hold to the country life they had found so good, but do so as working farmers not dependent on a job in town. They made the move in the faith that the land would repay them well for the care they proposed to give to its enrichment and upbuilding.

So it is a continuation of the adventure in living and in no sense an experiment station's economic report that unfolds in these following pages. Many and various hearts will vibrate to the notes that are struck as the months and the seasons wheel by. A naturalist himself, Len Hall writes not so much to others as expert as he as to the wider range of those who retain at least a trace of interest in the outdoors, in wildlife, in growing things. The interested novice—and that includes most of us—may find himself reaching for the handbook on birds or on wildflowers to help make more real and personal the journeys about the farm with Len and Ginnie. But whether or not the reader seeks it, some part of a broad liberal education on the outdoors is bound to rub off on him.

The author has capacity to see and to describe what he sees with simplicity and beauty. He "speaks to those on treadmills" not by preaching the joys and virtues of rural life but by sharing what he feels as life goes on about the farm. The humor and lightness of touch with which neighbors and animals are made to live for you blend with the soberness which marks such chapters as "Drought" and "Big Farms or Small?"

Above all, the book will have nostalgic appeal for those of whom it is said: "You may take the *boy* out of the *country*, but you can never take the *country* out of the *boy*."

The latter half of the years the Halls have spent on the Ozark farm were marked by continuous drought over the western part of the south central states, and the Bellevue valley in Missouri has not been spared. Their farming test has been made, I believe, under conditions more trying than normal. How have they made out? The concluding paragraphs sum up debits and credits, with stress on the debits as warning that flight to the land is no sure and easy cure for harassing economic and personal problems of the city family. The Halls strike their personal balance in the closing sentence:

"For our part, we have made our choice—and we would not trade our life at Possum Trot Farm for any other that we know."

preface

Possum Trot Farm lies in a high valley in the heart of the eastern Ozarks of Missouri. It is, by any standards one might set, a working farm, and we who live here and till the fields and tend the animals are working farmers. These are simple facts that can be attested to by many visitors who have come here during our ten years of residence, and with whom we have spent innumerable hours walking over the fields and talking of the things we have tried to accomplish. There have been farmers singly and in groups, scientists and technicians from the agricultural services, wildlife biologists, foresters—and just plain people with an interest in the land or in one or another of Nature's countless aspects. Most have left with us more of value than they have taken away.

While this book is in no sense a treatise on agriculture, it *is* a book about everyday living on a family-sized farm in a beautiful part of America. As is natural in such a book, you will find here many references to work in the fields throughout the year and also to our daily experiences with our animals. If you should miss from these references that sense of tragicomedy and of melodrama which marks so many country books, our excuse must be that we are professional rather than amateur farmers. As such we meet the everyday vicissitudes of farming as a matter of course.

Our aims through the years at Possum Trot Farm have been comparatively simple; to build steadily the fertility of our fields and woods, to market the produce of this land in the form of good livestock, and to accomplish these things against a background of living that seems to us worth while. It is chiefly with this country living that the book is concerned: with the swing of the seasons, the arrival and departure of songbirds and waterfowl, the wildflowers of spring and the color of autumn, the creatures, wild and tame, that make their homes with us—all these against the steady rhythm of the farmer's year.

Every book should have a purpose, though it be a modest one. If the pages that follow should bring to you some deeper understanding and appreciation of our natural world, of our relationship as human beings to it and our dependence upon it, of our responsibility for husbanding its resources and using them wisely, then I will be richly rewarded.

My thanks are due to the St. Louis *Post-Dispatch,* in whose columns much of this material first appeared in somewhat different form.

LEONARD HALL

Possum Trot Farm
Caledonia, Missouri

SPRING

march

A *Million Stars*

Can you remember it—the smell of wood smoke on a frosty March night? And you in unaccustomed Sunday knickerbockers, scratchy and less comfortable than overalls, trotting home from Epworth League—or was it Christian Endeavor—down the main street of some small country town.

Above your head, in the deep bowl of the sky, a million stars flickered like bright fireflies. Some seemed so near that almost you could touch them by reaching upward—and some so far that the vague word "infinite" took on meaning for you. And over against the western horizon, to guide you home, a great planet burned with a clear blue light.

Along that quiet street were no jangling tubes of neon in raw reds and greens. But friendly windows in small houses painted white glowed with the light of lamps on parlor tables. And now and then you would see a lantern, bobbing along toward barn or chicken house and sending immense shadows dancing ahead of it. Or if you were out toward the town's edge, perhaps it was the lantern of some countryman caught late in town and hurrying toward his farm.

No fumes of gasoline or smell of motor oil hung close along that street. But from each chimney tip curled friendly smoke, and sometimes you would know whether it was green oak burning in the stove, or hickory. On such a night the town dogs barked and most of them you knew. That one would be John Brown's old liver and white pointer—and Bill Nipper's big setter answering. Then if you listened hard, you would hear the sound that kept them both from going to sleep quietly beneath their respective porches. Far over on the wooded ridge just south of town, some hound was "barking treed." And once and again, on that trip home, you would have to detour into the dusty road, where some young buck had left his polished buggy hitched to a picket fence, his patient mare dozing between the shafts while he sparked comfortably beside the kitchen stove.

Perhaps when you reached home there was still one chore to round out the day. That would be to light your own lantern, with wick trimmed smooth, and head out to the barn to make sure Boss and her calf were bedded down safe for the night. And there would be the calf, curled in the deep straw of the box stall, his head tucked back along his side. Above him, contentedly chewing her cud, stood Boss; she turned her head to watch you gravely while you forked hay into the manger. The lantern cast long shadows across the dim recesses of the barn, and cobwebs swayed gently from the loft beams. There was rustling of mice overhead and a tangy fragrance that is the smell of cow's milk and summer hay and corn in the feed bins.

Strange how these memories come back clear; what small things start the chain that leads with unbroken links into the past. Last night it rained—the cold, raw rain of March—and I lit the kerosene lantern and went out late to the barn. Just that morning we had brought home three new white-faced cows with month-old calves at their sides. All day they had huddled in a corner of the pasture, waiting for the strangeness of their new home to wear away. It was almost bedtime when the rain began, and I was worried about whether the cows would have sense enough to take their calves into shelter. But I needn't have been concerned, for there were the three youngsters, tucked away safely in the warmest corner of the barn.

Today has been clear with a bright sun, but windy. The wind died at sunset and the temperature dropped. We went to supper at the home of our neighbors, Harry and Ethel Russell, and by the time we came back it was freezing. The sky was a mantle of stars, and in the west burned the great planet. Tiger and Mike came gladly to greet us, and in the air was the fragrance of wood smoke from the fire still burning on our hearth. Robert Coffin, the poet of Maine, once put it this way:

> And the spice of hay in mows,
> Of harness leather and of cows,
> Of musty oats and fodder can—
> Make a singer of a man.

Wild Geese

Though March brings many a murky day, there are signs by which we know that spring will not be long in coming. Snow may fall before the fruit trees blossom, yet there is promise in the buds of elm trees and the exquisite small flowers of the red maples. These appear long before the leaf buds: a circlet of five pollen flowers around the twig, red with tiny brown anthers at the ends of slender yellow filaments so that any slight air movement may set the pollen flying, and separate drooping flowers with spreading stamens which will eventually become the winged seeds. March is a time of winds and April of breezes that play their part in pollinating our trees, sometimes completing the process for all individuals of a single species within a matter of a day or two. This may be, in fact, one reason why we are seldom conscious of the flowering of trees with inconspicuous blossoms. The bloom appears, disburses its pollen, withers, and is gone before we are conscious of it.

A spring songster that we heard on a clear evening last week, as we walked out to the pasture to watch the young calves playing, was the sweet-voiced white-throated sparrow, which arrives in our valley on about March fifth and can be

counted on to serenade us each evening until mid-May. "Old Sam Peabody—Peabody—Peabody" is the rhyme generally given for the white-throat's song, though nothing could come further from translating its indescribable and fragile beauty. The small bird is one of the handsomest of the twenty-six varieties of sparrows that migrate northward through the Mississippi Valley; it can be readily marked by its black crown divided by a white stripe; another broad stripe over the eye, which starts as yellow and fades into white; and finally the pure-white throat patch that gives the bird its name. The song has variations in melody, though not in number of notes.

Many of the waterfowl and shore birds are moving up the flyway and each day from now on will find new ones stopping at the ponds. There will be the cormorant and, if we are as lucky as last year, perhaps the common loon. The little pied-billed grebe will drop in for a visit and the green-winged teal, which is one of the first ducks to head north. Then will come the sora rail and yellowlegs, the sandpipers, and finally, on some clear day, we'll hear the golden plover high above the valley, making its leisurely spring flight from the pampas of the Argentine to a land above the Arctic Circle where summer days are short and where it will build its nest on the mossy tundra and raise its long-legged chicks.

Another band of migrants that never fails to thrill us is the skein of geese—they may be blues or snow geese, white-fronted, or the great Canadas—cleaving the high air above the valley on swift and certain wings. Be it a clear March morning or a misty night when clouds blanket the mountain, there is one sound that never fails to bring us out under the sky. For the crying of the wild geese heading for Hudson's Bay is the certainty that spring has arrived. In autumn their passage is swift and high, as if they knew that each bit of marsh and pond and stream bank was lined with lethal guns. By the same token, the northbound honkers seem to realize that spring is the season of truce, when they may spread out over the flyway, stop for a while at any likely pond to harvest a night's meal from an adjoining wheat field, or pick up corn left from the autumn harvest.

The blue geese were long mistakenly called brant by most Midwesterners, and blue geese were considered to be quite rare. Now we know that the brant is a separate and smaller species, commonly found on both east and west coasts, but seen only as a casual here in our central states. The blue goose is now recognized as having a very distinct flight pattern, from nesting grounds high above the Arctic Circle on islands north of the continental land mass to a wintering area on the coasts of Louisiana and Texas, where the entire flight seems to concentrate during the cold months. When the northward migration starts, it is a magnificent sight to watch countless thousands of the big birds concentrating around the junction of the Missouri and Platte at this season of the year.

Although Possum Trot lies at a considerable distance from any large river, we see a surprising number of waterfowl during this spring migration—a much larger number, in fact, than comes through each autumn. Among these, in past years, have always been the blue geese, including a pair that stopped for two weeks last spring at the Big Pond. These gradually lost their fear, so that even when they were feeding in the wheat fields we could approach to within thirty or forty yards of them. But last week a band of blue geese, accompanied by four of the beautiful white snow geese, gave us a real thrill. I was at work in the shop, and Ginnie in her kitchen, when we heard them calling close overhead. We came rushing out together, to find the big birds circling confusedly above the barn lot and so low that it seemed one might almost reach up and touch them. There were seventy-five or more in the band, and we watched them drift over toward the mountain, then suddenly make up their minds to land. They circled again, dropped their wings into a rigid, down-swept position, and came to rest in our bottom field.

Although there was rain in the air and a strong wind blowing, Ginnie and I pulled on boots and coats, took binoculars, and hurried out to the car. Once down the lane, we parked out of sight and moved carefully along the fence row. The geese were well out in the field and apparently just resting, for there was little food to be had in the brown pasture. Some members of the flock dozed while others preened themselves. The four snow geese seemed more alert, craning their necks and with their heads turned always in our direction. We could not come very close, for they were right in the center of the field. Now and then one would flap its wings and mount a few feet into the air, only to settle down again; and once the whole flock took alarm at a car coming down the lane. They rose into the air, circled for a few moments, then came down again in the very same spot. Undoubtedly they could see us all the time; yet except for maintaining their watchfulness, they seemed not at all disturbed.

The rain came down harder, and we were just about to leave, when we heard more geese calling. Off to northward came another band, this time perhaps twenty. Our flock murmured among themselves, then sent out a honk or two of invitation. The new flock broke the pattern of their flight and drifted about in confusion for several moments. But somehow this was not the place they wanted to rest, for after a while they reformed their "V" and disappeared into the clouds that obscured the crest of Buford. The interesting thing is that all these geese were moving southward instead of north; and sure enough, that night the thermometer started to drop. The wind blew half a gale and by morning the mercury stood at 16°. But our geese remained for several hours. After we had finished feeding that evening and Matt was starting home, we heard them again and were just in time to see the big band disappearing to southward, with the four snow geese conspicuous in the flock.

It is easy to distinguish the blue geese from their big cousins, the Canadas, for the latter are nearly twice as large. The Canada, moreover, has a much longer neck, which is black with a white collar band. The blue goose gets its name from the bluish-gray color of the wings, and has a dusky gray body and a white head and neck. The snow goose seems to stand taller than the blue and is, as its name implies, pure white except for the "trailing edge" of the primary wing feathers, which are black. The Midwestern member of the family is not highly regarded as a bird for the table; yet its numbers have been greatly reduced, even as have those of the fish-eating ducks, by overshooting and destruction of resting and feeding grounds along the flyways.

Geese travel in family flocks; but when they have stopped to rest or feed on the spring migration, there will always be a number of lone birds moving restlessly about the outskirts of the band. Often we have noticed this, but it took naturalist Aldo Leopold to confirm that these were single survivors of families which went south together last autumn. With some of his students, Aldo kept records for many years and showed that flocks of six or multiples of six occurred too often to be accidental. These were, indeed, family groups and the lone birds are those whose families have fallen to the hunters' guns. Whether or not they breed again is a matter of doubt, for there are many records of Canadas in captivity that lose their mates to some accident and will not nest again. So we may grieve for the lone geese, calling disconsolately as they search the vast skyways in vain, yet pulled to the northland by an urge that is older than the race of man.

No Other Life

On the last rainy week end we mapped out tasks that lay ahead of us during spring and summer. These we set down in our "Balanced Farming Workbook," which contains the soil maps and field maps of the farm. In the pages of the book we list work to be done in each field: mechanical practices, such as terracing, building waterways, and planting fences of multiflora rose; the seeding to various crops and amounts of lime and fertilizer to be used; the approximate dates of pasturing or harvest. All of these point toward the eventual goal of a ten-year plan, and the total list reminds me of a story Bill Colman told last time he was at the farm. An old farmer Bill knew during his boyhood was in the habit of getting up at a quarter to four each morning. That was a bit extreme, even for a farmer. But when asked why he did it, the old fellow had a ready answer. "Well," he said, "when I don't get up that early the first thing I know it's six o'clock, and not a thing done."

Ginnie and I can't make it quite at four o'clock, yet neither do we need worry about daylight-saving time. We will save all the daylight we can and keep things going from sun to sun and still have plenty left to do tomorrow. That's life on a farm. And still, when friends ask whether the effort is worth while, we can give them an honest answer. With considerable experience to go on, we can say that there is no other life for which we would trade. Nor do I have difficulty in setting down the reasons. First and foremost, I would put the close and constant contact with nature and the outdoors. This does not mean a life of peace and quiet such as some city dwellers dream about. There are always plenty of problems—watching the spring calf crop for all the diseases of childhood, the fields for erosion, the hay in the barn lest it all be fed out before grass time, seed and fertilizer to have on hand for sowing, machinery to make ready for busy days ahead. But even when going about these tasks one can watch and appreciate the sunrise and sunset and the swing of the seasons.

We would have a hard time returning to the indoor life of the city with its manufactured excitements, its nervous tensions, its lack of any except artificial forms of physical exercise. Too much of the activity that we remember still seems lacking in deep conviction and purpose, nor could we content ourselves again with the worship of bigness for its own sake and of gadgetry as an end in itself, which seems an inseparable part of American city living. Perhaps the values we find here are no greater, nor our accomplishments more worth while; yet at least the former do not change and the latter are the work of our own hands. Even contacts with our neighbors are on a basis of mutual helpfulness such as has almost disappeared from urban life. When a job comes along that we can't handle alone, and there are a good many of them, we are seldom at a loss because there is always a neighbor willing to take time from his own busy day to pitch in with us and get that job done. Thus it was last week when Joe and Junior Ricketts came to help dehorn the young calves before we put them out on pasture with the cows.

The week brought other visitors. Giff Adams of the Forest Service came from Fredericktown to tell us about the national convention of the beekeepers, down in Biloxi. And we talked of the showers that have ended what might have been a disastrous season of spring forest fires in Missouri. Now that the state and national forest services are working together, fire control is becoming even more effective. Here in our community, Joe Ricketts and his boys have taken over the job of working with the State Forestry Service to investigate and fight fires, something that will eventually mean fewer flash floods on our streams and more forest revenue for our county. On another rainy afternoon Jim Connelly visited us. His work for the Boy Scouts, for the forests of Missouri, and other community causes make Jim one of our most valuable citizens. But he is rich in other attainments as well, for he is naturalist, fisherman, canoeist, all-round outdoorsman, and scholar. Jim brought a present under his arm, a wrenhouse fashioned from a hollow log, and his copy of *Possum Trot Farm* to be autographed. I was delighted to find the margins of the book filled with annotations by the reader, a sign of interest in the contents.

Another visitor was our friend Norman White, who is our neighbor to the north. There he farms his ancestral acres, raises good shorthorn cattle, and now and then stops by to discuss the state of the crops and weather. Norman can get to the very back of his farm most easily by driving down the county road past our house and then up the lane on the far side of the creek. He had been up there digging sassafras roots to send to friends in California, where I have no doubt they are brewed into tea at this season to thicken the blood of folks who must live in that enervating climate. The truth is, I'm a bit vague about the benefits of sassafras tea, yet I well remember its aromatic fragrance and pleasant sensation on the palate when my great-aunt Lucy used to make it each spring.

Norman told us that not only had he seen the tracks of the deer reported recently, but also on two successive days had watched the deer themselves browsing at the edge of an old field. There were four of them: a big doe, a spike buck, a yearling, and a fawn of this season. We're reporting them to our Conservation Agent, Cleval Corey of Ironton, and to the agent at Potosi, so everything possible can be done to see that they come to no harm. This increase in our various forms of wildlife is a matter for real satisfaction. It is also proof that better methods of land use—in this case, protection of the timber against fire and the progress of soil conservation in our county—mean a better environment for the wild creatures as well as for man.

The Lost Calf

The longer one works with animals, caring for them and observing them closely, the more certain one is to become anthropomorphic. This one-dollar word does not describe a dread tropical disease. It merely means that one attributes to animals the characteristics of human beings. Some people seem to do this more readily than others. The thing is difficult to explain, and I am not even certain it has to do with familiarity with the animals in question, for I find many country folk who work with animals every day and develop little interest in and certainly no affection for them. I know many a farm dog that is well fed and never abused, yet never gets a pat on the head or an invitation to come in beside the fire on a cold night. There are barn cats and house cats around most farms that receive their quota of milk in return for catching mice, yet live totally anonymous lives. They never have names, and when the tabbys have produced a sufficient number of offspring they are eliminated by time-honored methods for getting rid of excess cats. Even the family cow, which must be fed and milked twice a day the year round, does not become a part of the family.

It isn't like that at Possum Trot, worse luck. When we get a message, be it letter or phone call or telegram, which means we must be away from the farm for a day or two, Mike knows its contents at least as well as we do. Tiger knows, too, but is a bit more philosophical. An Irish setter reflects moods as an April sky reflects weather. In the hunting season it is impatience or, if we've made a round of the fields, content. If it is company—and the company happens to be one of our hunting companions, regardless of time of year—it is a dignified desire to have his head rubbed and an expression that has caused Ran Barrett to rename old Mike "the Judge." Chester Davis has suggested, on the basis of his nobility of expression on such occasions, that we should run Michael for the United States Senate. Certainly he has the mien. But when we have to go away from the farm overnight, his expression would break anyone's heart.

How anyone can deal with a cow on the occasion of the

arrival of a new calf and not believe that animals are at least half human is beyond me. Cows have their own methods of taking care of these matters, just as do Esquimo women and those of the South Sea Islands. They instinctively find a sheltered and comfortable spot, although too often it is not the easiest place for the human being who is also interested in finding the calf. The cow knows how to hide the calf, just as wild animals do, so that once it has been thoroughly licked dry and fed, she can go away to graze. Cows are fiercely protective, ready to defend their young against all comers. Once the calf is hidden, they will go through all sorts of subterfuges to keep you from finding it until it is large enough to stand up for itself with the other baby calves and can safely join the herd. Their concern is constant; the newspapers are filled with accounts of human mothers who don't do half as good a job.

It is when something happens to a baby calf, however, that you know the mother cow has something very close to human feeling or emotion. While we were away last week, a new baby calf arrived. We left on Friday morning and it came that night. Matt was pretty sure on Saturday morning that it had been born; but this cow is partially blind in one eye, which inclines her to be wild, and we knew from previous experience that she will not hesitate to charge anyone who comes near her newborn calf. More than this, she will play hide and seek with you for hours to keep you from finding where she has hidden it. So while Matt looked for it on Saturday, the cow gave him no help and he finally abandoned the search. When I fed in the evening, she came to the barn and I knew for the first time that the calf had arrived, though she did not bring it in with her. She seemed, in fact, worried. Her bag was full of milk as though the calf might not have fed for many hours. She made short side trips out of the barn lot and bawled incessantly. I made as much of a search as possible before dark, then had to give up, since she could have hidden the calf anywhere on two hundred acres. But I did not worry too much, for she is a fine big cow and this was her second calf.

It was after I went to bed that I really began to worry. That old girl seemed to stand as close to the bedroom window as she could get. There she bawled and bawled as if her heart was broken. It seemed certain her calf must have been lost through one disaster or another. The creek was in flood and she might have tried to bring the tiny thing across. Or it might have been born dead. Anything, in fact, might have happened. The clock struck eleven and then twelve, though I knew there was nothing I could do until daylight. Finally I went to sleep and dreamed about drowning calves. At a quarter to six I was up, made a cup of coffee, tossed out hay for the sixty head of cattle at the big barn and corn for the mares, and started my search.

I hiked along the bluff to the north boundary of the farm, then back along the creek. Together with Mike and Tiger we searched every thicket. Tiger has an insatiable interest in newborn calves, while Mike points them from a respectable distance. But we hunted in vain. By now the cows had come out along the ridge, and again the mother of the lost calf bawled incessantly. Finally, as I worked along the bank of the flooded stream, I heard a husky "bla-a-a-t" from the woods on the opposite side. Though the water was swift and deep, I plunged in with the dogs following and, a moment later, found a fine healthy calf hidden behind a fallen log. There was no doubt it was hungry, so I picked it up and waded back, while it bawled lustily at every step.

Once across, it started for the other cows, which nuzzled it curiously, and finally followed them clear to the top of the bluff. It was a strong young fellow or it could never have negotiated the steep path. Once on top, I felt certain the mother would find it, so I went on about the business of the day. I am still not certain whether she did or whether she spent the day searching in vain on the other side of the stream; for late that evening the calf followed the other cows to the barn, bawling loudly, and the mother was not with it. After feeding, I called and called and evidently brought her in, for an hour later, when I went to the barn for a last look, the calf was at her side. She took one look at me and chased me round the barn at a sixty-mile clip, shaking her head furiously as though the whole thing had been my fault. If I had not forgotten my stick, I would have been tempted to whack her for having wasted my entire Sunday.

Making Beef

Frequently friends from the city gaze at our cows and calves loafing in the sun in the pastures or munching hay at the barn and say, "What a wonderful way to get rich, just sitting around watching a big bunch of beef animals putting on pounds."

An antidote for this impression could easily be gained by following a cattleman through a typical week or, for that matter, by going over his books at the end of the year. For a lot more goes into your beefsteak than some contented fellow sitting on his porch smoking his pipe while cattle turn grass, hay, and grain into meat.

One day last week, for example, a phone call came from Dr. Sheets, our veterinarian. Given good weather, he said, he would be over early on Friday morning to vaccinate our "shotes" against cholera. I told him we would make a morning of it and take this opportunity to get the calves ready for summer. There were a half-dozen heifer calves to vaccinate against Bang's disease, the baby calves to shoot for blackleg and to dehorn, a bunch of fall calves to dehorn and ear-tag, and the whole lot to dust against the mites and lice that seem inevitably to collect in their woolly coats during the winter months.

A lot of cattlemen are going to ask whether we really need the veterinarian for all of these tasks, and the answer is that we can vaccinate and dehorn as well as anybody. But the Bang's inoculation should be given by a veterinarian so that the calves can be tattooed in the ear and the vaccination registered, in case you want to sell the heifer. It doesn't pay us to buy cholera serum for two pigs, and we wanted to use the new serum that prevents any possibility of spreading future cholera on the farm. Moreover, if we had to bring in the whole herd and cut out a calf or two every time one needed some small attention, we would never get anything else done. And finally, by saving up everything that is not an emergency, we have a chance to go over the whole herd with Dr. Sheets three or four times a year, and at the same time to get all the necessary work done safely and expertly and with a minimum of lost time.

So we were up and had the feeding done early on Friday morning; then brought all of the cows and calves down to the stable yard behind the house. Next the whole lot were driven into the cutting pens to be separated. All of the fall calves went into the back pen, while their mothers were cut out and sent to the nearby pasture, where they stood and bawled loudly. Then the cows with baby calves were placed in the front pen so they could be got out of the way first. We set up our operating table beside the stanchion and were ready when Dr. Sheets drove into the yard at nine o'clock.

Buckets were filled with warm water and disinfectant. Ear tags and the special pliers with which they are attached were laid out. Then came a row of serums and hypodermic needles, the tattoo marker and dye, the dehorning paste for the baby calves, and Barnes dehorners for the larger ones. The benzine hexachloride powder for dusting against mites and lice was made ready. Then we went to work. Handling the baby calves is easy. Matt runs them into a corner and catches them. With the hypodermic we give them their blackleg shot, cheap insurance against a deadly disease that can kill the finest young animal in a matter of hours from the time it strikes. Then we clip the hair from around the horn bud, scratch it with a knife or file, and apply the paste that keeps the horn from ever forming. A good coating of vaseline is smeared around this to keep the caustic from running in case of rain. Then the baby is ready to return to its mother who is bawling outside the pen.

The larger calves must be run into the chute, one at a time, and their heads fastened in the stanchion. Here the heifers get their Bang's vaccination, this being a disease that sometimes wipes out whole herds and, when present in dairy cows, causes undulant fever in human beings. Matt runs the animals into the chute, I catch their heads, Dr. Sheets "shoots" them, Matt dusts them with BHC, Dr. Sheets tattoos the left ear and Matt applies the dye, I clip in the ear tag, Dr. Sheets operates the dehorning shears, I apply the disinfectant, and the calf is ready to go back to the herd.

At eleven-thirty we finished the calves and were ready for the pigs. As Matt and I held the barrow in the air by his hind legs for Dr. Sheets to shoot with his hypodermic, it squealed as if it were being killed. The gilt rushed up and gave Matt a good bite in the leg. "Just like a woman," he said, and ruefully rubbed the bite. We applied disinfectant all around and Ginnie called us for dinner. Are we, as some agricultural authorities obviously believe, "rugged individualists" enough to keep this up for long when every calf we raise has a good chance of showing a fifty-dollar loss? When one of the top agricultural economists in America told us recently that when farm prices were at their peak five years ago, American wage earners worked fewer hours to feed their families better than ever in history? These are interesting questions for a farmer, at least, to ponder.

Country Adventures

Since the weather has warmed up, Mike has abandoned his bed on the porch to curl up in the leaves outside our bedroom window. The arrangement is well enough for him, since it enables his sensitive nose to catch whatever scent is floating on

the night air and his almost equally sensitive ears to hear what farmers' dogs are barking, up and down the valley. But it doesn't work quite so well for us. If either the sound or the scent seems to old Mike worth investigating, he goes charging out of his bed with a roar and a few minutes later can be heard barking away down on the creek or from the top of the bluff behind the house. What starts him off may be the hounds running, far off to the east on Buford Mountain, or the strange squalling bark of a vixen fox, or the scent of a nocturnally wandering raccoon or opossum.

One night last week, just after we were asleep, Mike woke us with a single loud bark, which was abruptly choked off in the middle. This time Tiger was sleeping in the yard with him and he, too, let out one yelp. We sat up in bed just in time to be almost knocked flat by the overpowering aroma of skunk. Before I could close the storm sash and drop the window, the odor pervaded every room in the house. We heard the dogs come in to their beds on the back porch and had only to open the kitchen door to realize that their malodorous friend had managed to drench them both. Nor had they done him any harm, apparently, for a search of the yard by moonlight showed no corpse, and after the air had cleared, a faint scent on the night breeze told us he had gone his unhurried way. As for the dogs, they lived in disgrace outdoors for several days, finally becoming unobjectionable except when they were wet.

On a recent walk, we were accompanied as usual by Mike and Tiger, who ranged far ahead and investigated every brush pile and hollow tree. Now and then they would bounce out a cottontail that would lead them a merry chase along the bluff until it tired of the sport and dived into the safety of a ground-hog hole. Nuisance, the barn cat, also came along, for there is nothing he likes better than a jaunt through the woods.

There was a time when old Veronica joined us on these junkets, but nowadays she prefers to stay at home, curled beside the fire. Nuisance follows us in fits and starts, bouncing along for a while and then stopping to rest or investigate a field-mouse nest. When he falls behind, he complains bitterly, yet will not be picked up and carried. To watch him crossing the wet ground beneath the bluff is a circus—picking up each foot and setting it down with the greatest of care in the driest spot he can find, and telling us every moment exactly what he thinks of people who like to tramp through the mud.

As we came back to do the evening chores, we found the

cattle lying on the high ground contentedly chewing their cuds. Nuisance by this time had fallen far behind. Looking back, we saw him stalking along through the herd, and we stopped to watch. A half dozen of the big steers got to their feet, and surrounded the cat in a circle. Nuisance, in no wise disconcerted, arched his back and rubbed against the nose of the nearest one. This must have tickled, for the big steer bunted him gently, then reached out his long tongue and licked the cat behind the ear. By now the whole forty head were on their feet and surrounding the cat, some of the smaller heifers playfully lowering their heads and charging in as though to toss him over the nearest fence. When progress was too badly impeded, Nuisance simply lay down and crossed his paws, upon which all the cattle reached out their noses for a sniff. Then a space opened up and the cat proceeded unconcernedly toward us, still pausing to arch his back and rub against whatever animal was nearest.

It was almost as though he were holding court with these great creatures that towered like giants above him, and the cattle, for all their curiosity, were also somewhat awed. Thinking about it afterward, we wondered whether he wasn't actually already good friends with them from nocturnal journeyings to the barn to hunt mice.

This relationship between the animals is one of the most interesting things on the farm. Often we see Ribbon, who has been perfectly trained as a cattle horse, rubbing noses over the barn-lot fence with a steer. When we are riding, Tiger follows along so close behind that the iron shoes of the mare miss his nose by a hairbreadth; yet never once has he been kicked or stepped on. One of the steers loves to chase old Mike and will go after him, kicking and bucking like a colt, whenever the dog appears in the pasture.

All of the cattle are as curious about Tiger as about the cat;

but Tiger doesn't reciprocate their desire to become better acquainted, and generally takes refuge between my feet when we are about the barn or in the pasture. Of them all, it is Nuisance who believes he is generally loved, so that we are apt to find him curled up in the horse manger or sharing a bed on a cold night with either of the dogs, who seem to tolerate rather than enjoy his company.

Brisk Bidding

In any livestock country, the weekly auction sale is a big event. Especially at this season of the year, and on a rainy day when work outdoors is impossible, the farmers gather from far and near. With a good many of them livestock trading is part of the business of farming; with others a farm is merely a place to run hogs and cattle between trades. And there are a fair number who fall into neither of these categories. They come to the sale to visit with friends from the more distant valleys, to buy some shoats or a milk cow, or merely to listen to the bidding and see how prices are running this week. Tuesday is sale day at the Caledonia auction barn; Potosi holds its sale on Saturday and Farmington on Wednesday.

We do not go regularly, being neither traders nor often in the market for livestock. But once in a while, on a rainy afternoon, Matt and I drop over to Caledonia to see what is going on—and we always enjoy ourselves. Last week the trucks were lined up along the highway for half a mile, the pens were full of stock, and the bidding went along briskly.

If you intend buying cattle, hogs, horses, or mules at the country sale, you should have your wits about you. In addition to animals that have been consigned by local farmers, there will be a big percentage of stock brought in by traders from the surrounding countryside, and also by the company that operates this particular sale barn.

The bidding is started by one of the ring men, opening at a figure close to the absolute bottom price at which the animal or lot of animals can be sold. It generally moves too fast to be followed by anyone in the crowd unless he has spent a lot of time following the sales. It is next to impossible to tell whether bids are from bona fide buyers or from "company" bidders. Many a lot will be knocked down at a good round figure only to appear next day at another sale. In such cases, the top outside bid was not high enough to suit the "company," which carried the price up merely to encourage the bidding on the next lot. Sometimes this works, for it is often hard to tell whether or not a genuine sale had been consummated.

Trading is the lifeblood of the country, and the buyer who pretends to know anything about the business is bound to take his chances. "Sharp as a razor" is a term of approval, and the taking of any sucker is an entirely legitimate part of the deal. As a matter of fact, this is as true of trading over the barnyard fence as it is in the auction ring, except that in the latter case time is of the essence. A man who is in the business day in and day out needs infinite patience, a frank and open face, and a line of blarney with which to distract your attention from the fallen hock, the weak hindquarters, the worn-down teeth, or other—to him—quite unimportant blemishes of the wares he has to offer.

By the same token, when he comes to look at your fine cattle, he allows his imagination full play. He wants you to name your price; protests that to buy at such a figure would bankrupt him. Ask for his ideas about value and he's just ashamed, he says, even to mention the figure he had in mind. Maybe he'd better head on home. But don't let that worry you. The day is young, and this is the trader's business, and if by late afternoon he has clinched a deal that he figures has shown him a profit, the day has been well spent. As one of them put it, not long ago, "I'd rather lose five dollars on a deal than let a day go by without making a trade."

The good trader needs more than shrewdness and a knowledge of human nature. He must also be an expert judge of livestock. And this applies most of all at those times of year when the stock is looking its worst. Is this cow thin because she's "agey" or because she has made it through the winter on rough fodder? Is she likely to bring a good calf and then fatten

up on summer pasture to turn a fair profit, or is she one of those barren, bony hulks that is bound to result in a loss? The trader must know prices and demand. It helps, as well, if he knows who has an extra crib of corn or barn loft full of hay and may need extra stock to eat it. By the same token, he will do well to know whose feed supply is running thin and what farms are overstocked with cattle when the pasture gets short. Knowledge of such conditions may lead to bargains or profits.

If you are a beginner at the livestock business, an experienced trader is apt to give you what you want—sound animals at the going rate. You will get honest treatment, but the fun will have gone out of the transaction for the country trader. There is just one mistake to avoid: never pretend to a knowledge you don't have—never, that is, unless you want to be taken for a trimming with fluted edges and ruffles.

There remains, of course, the occasional trader who is not farsighted enough to know there is more than one way of doing business. Often he does not realize that his prospective customer is used to dealing in markets where the seller quotes one price for an honest product and the buyer either accepts it at that price or turns it down. Or the prospect may figure he cannot give a day's time to the pleasant bantering involved in so many country transactions. He is used to figuring time as money. The best answer here, I think, is to spread a clear understanding around the countryside as to where you stand. Being neither a horse trader nor an expert in the merchandise, you will trust the seller. If he trims you once, you will find someone else with whom to do business thereafter. Most traders will forgo the pleasure of barter for the assurance of a solid and lasting business connection.

april

Wondrous Awakening

When is the beginning of this magic season we call spring? There is a stodgy date on the calendar that proclaims it as March twenty-first. But sometimes spring comes earlier, and sometimes that day finds the countryside still wrapped in snow and vernal breezes many weeks away. The hope is always with us that this is the year of an early spring, for the heart in time rebels against the cold and longs for budding trees and the green of meadows and young lambs leaping in the fields with the joy of being alive.

Part of its wayward charm lies in the very unpredictability of this coy maiden among the seasons. There are years when we are conscious of strange stirrings in the earth almost as soon as the days start lengthening perceptibly, with twilight lasting just a moment or two longer each evening. The weather turns warm and is followed by rain that sends the snow scurrying. Though it is just above freezing, we will hear, as we finish up the chores after dark, the singing of spring peepers. Years of country experience tell us this cannot be the real thing; that sap of trees is still deep in the roots, that no seeds are stirring, and that the groundhog sleeps soundly in his burrow.

Perhaps two weeks later comes another sunny day. And

this time Ginnie wants to know if it isn't time to take down the storm sash, bring out the lawn furniture, and fix up the west porch where we eat all summer long. I point out that in other years we have found it uncomfortably cold to start having our meals outdoors until perhaps the third week in May, and that we will be sitting indoors around the fireplace for another two months.

Even our animals are, I think, subject to this magic of spring. They browse out in the almost-bare fields and find a few sprigs of wild onion that have come up ahead of the season. Soon, we have to go out and drive the cows in for their evening meal of hay and grain, which has suddenly become dull and uninteresting fare. For the hunter, the day comes when he hears geese flying north; and for the farmer, the time when he feels the earth and decides it is dry enough to plow his oats ground.

Anglers are especially susceptible. Soon after New Year's you find them varnishing rods and tightening ferrules, taking reels apart to be oiled, looking over lines and lures, and spending noon hours in the sporting-goods stores. Trout fishermen are the worst of this breed. Sure as it sleets on March first, you will find them lined along the bank of some roiled and muddy stream, perhaps two hundred miles from home, elbow to elbow with dozens of brother anglers, hopefully casting a Black Gnat or McGinty or even a lowly garden hackle.

For my part, I would not try to set a certain day for spring's arrival. It is more an accumulation of signs and portents, sometimes coming reluctantly and sometimes in a headlong rush. All the signs finally add up unmistakably to rebirth and awakening. It is a time for playing hooky, for spending hours afield when there is nothing more important to do than to observe and contemplate. It is a certainty that is still uncertain—a beginning and a promise, a wonderful recurring moment in life.

Time of Singing

April is a month when each day brings some fresh sign of the advancing season. Thus there was a sunny morning last week when the clear whistle of bobwhite rang like a welcome from the front yard and we looked out to see the handsome cock quail, in his smart brown herringbone attire and white head stripes, perched on the fence. And on a balmy evening, sitting in the yard before supper, we hear the soft call of the mourning dove, the surest sign for the mountain people that frost is over and corn-planting time at hand.

This is, of course, the sound referred to in the Psalm: "And the voice of the turtle . . ." which actually is a Persian wild cousin of our dove with the name *tur-tur*. The Psalm from the Songs of Solomon is certainly among the loveliest expressions of the season: "For, lo! the winter is past, the rain is over and gone; the flowers appear on the earth; the time of the singing of birds is at hand and the voice of the turtle is heard in our land."

This is also the peak season in the northward migration of shorebirds, and one that we see in increasing numbers is the Wilson's snipe, commonly called jack snipe. This little fellow, as its name, *Capella delicata,* indicates, has been for centuries considered a table delicacy, a fact that almost led to its extinction by hunters. But for once the game authorities acted in time and a federal closed season for several years seems to be producing a goodly build-up in population. Now the limiting factor is probably the drainage of low, boggy land, which this bird prefers to open water. The Wilson's snipe is a small grayish-brown bird of about the same size as the woodcock and with the same short legs and long bill, although with a slimmer body. Since it feeds on such insects as crane flies, locusts, and grasshoppers, as well as worms and underground larvae, we are always glad to see it in our fields.

Often when we are working in the lower land, which is wet at this season, Mike and Tiger flush small bands of a half-dozen snipe. They rise in swift and erratic flight, uttering a reiterated "scaip, scaip" that is familiar to every gunner. Until one unlocks the secret of this darting flight, the small birds make difficult targets. At this time of year, we notice that if we stand still after the birds flush they often make a wide circle or two, high in the air, then drop down again to within a dozen feet of their starting point.

Two other interesting and, for our locality, rare birds that we have seen recently are the tiny sora rail and the American bittern. The sora rail is a strange little fellow, barely six inches long and among the smallest of its group. It nests close to the marsh and when flushed by the dogs is extremely reluctant to fly; in fact, it runs swiftly through the long grass and does not take to wing at all unless hard-pushed. Its slate-colored coat and small size are in sharp contrast to the big king and clapper rails, which attain a size of fifteen to twenty inches. The American bittern, on the other hand, is a large, stocky brown bird that somewhat resembles its cousin, the yellow-crowned night heron. However, in common with the least bittern, it is characterized by its curious posture when at rest, with the head and bill pointed upward as though it had a stiff neck.

The warm weather of recent days has brought out a host of wildflowers, many of which we had thought damaged by the cold spell. Dogwood is beginning to bloom and will be at its peak between now and early May. Some of the plum thickets are turning white. And in the woods is an endless variety of flowers: May apple, larkspur, anemone, false rue, yellow bellwort, and great beds of bluebells. If you are planning a spring trip into the country to see the blossoms, April is the time to make it. But if you go to the woods, where most of the flowers bloom, you will be well advised to take along an insect repellent. As for us, we stay at home and watch the advancing season. Often in the evening, after a day in the fields and when the milking is finished, we sit on the east terrace to enjoy a toddy before supper. I whistle a bobwhite into the yard, a mocking-bird sings softly from the multiflora hedge, and a brown thrasher with nesting material in its bill comes silently into the barberry bushes beside us. Nearby, the pie-cherry tree is white with blossoms and in one corner of the garden early lettuce and radishes are large enough to make a showing. Far down across the creek in the lower pasture, a long line of cows and calves goes slowly in single file, and out in the stable lot Daisy and Ribbon nicker and lean across the fence to nip the budding leaves from Ginnie's Concord grapes. It is an hour of enchantment, when we are likely to forget that dollars and power are the American criteria for success—or, if we do remember it, to decide that America has traded her birthright for a mess of pottage.

Woodcock

Through the center of our farm, from south to north, flows Saline Creek, and on down to join Cedar and Reed Creeks a half mile below. It is, like most others of the Ozark country, a stream of varying terrain and infinite variety. Where it enters the southern boundary it is broad, peaceful, and shallow, moving gently between low, wooded banks. But when water comes rolling down after a rain from the fire-scarred granite sides of Buford Mountain or from the gullying fields of farms higher up the watershed, it goes on a rampage. At one point, where our bottom fields had been plowed right up to the bank with no protecting margin of woodland cover, the stream bursts its bounds and sends a muddy torrent down across the land.

You would hardly believe, along in mid-August when

some stretches actually disappear into the gravel, that Saline could carry a devastating flood. Yet we have seen it rise ten feet in a few hours and go pouring through that good field carrying great tree trunks on its crest, cutting channels thirty feet wide and four feet deep, and then leaving these choked with hundreds of tons of sand and gravel. Such is the power of water running unchecked from the surface to the land.

The west boundary of the creek is an eighty-foot bluff, the abrupt end of the "Hagerstown limestone" soil of which our valley is so proud, but which we have let wash away through careless farming this past hundred years.

At the north end of the farm, where Saline crosses into the White place, there is an abrupt change in terrain and soil type. Here the creek plunges at once between two granite hills to form one of the "shut-ins" or small canyons typical of the streams of this region. There is some residual limestone here, for good red cedar grows on the steep hillsides. But on the whole there is a sharp line of demarcation between the plants that grow on the limestone and the acid-tolerant species of the granitic soils.

At this season, hiking along the creek, we can be certain of flushing a woodcock or two. A small butterball of a bird somewhat larger than our bobwhite, the woodcock is bright reddish-brown in color, with three dark stripes across its head and an extremely long, flexible bill. While it is known to nest in Missouri, we see it mainly as a migrant; and then not too often, since it slips along through the cover of creek banks and seldom flies at a height of more than thirty feet. Woodcock travel singly, although following closely the same route. This is why, in either autumn or spring, you can generally flush a bird or two from the same bit of cover, day after day, as long as the migration lasts. For me there has always been a fascination about the flight of the woodcock. When flushed it rises swiftly, sometimes as silently as an owl, but sometimes with a whistling sound produced by the wing primaries.

Maine and Ontario are the great nesting grounds for the bird, but Michigan, Wisconsin, and Minnesota all have a fair share. Practically the entire woodcock population seems to winter in Louisiana, but the flight patterns are not too well known and it seems likely that our birds are those which summer directly north of us. Certainly, if the birds of Maine and eastern Canada came this far north before heading for the Atlantic seaboard, we would see more of them as they passed through.

Like many other birds, the woodcock carry on an extremely interesting courtship performance, which I had the luck to observe in Wisconsin many springs ago. Arrived at the nesting area, the male woodcock selects a "singing ground" where the courtship ceremony takes place. This is generally an opening in the thicket or the edge of a field close to the nesting and feeding territory, and here, each day at dawn and dusk during April and early May, the "sky dance" of the male bird takes place. To see it, you must arrive early, select a good place for observation, and sit quietly. Presently the male will fly in from his feeding cover and the performance starts with a throaty note not unlike that of the nighthawk. Then the woodcock takes to the air, rising in wide spirals for perhaps three hundred feet and making a musical twittering as he goes. From this height he comes tumbling to earth like a falling leaf, singing with a liquid warble, to alight on the singing ground at exactly the spot where he took off. Here the bird struts, as do many others during courtship, all the time uttering the harsh "peentting" sound that is well known to every outdoorsman who lives in woodcock country. Again and again the flight is repeated, until daylight follows dawn or darkness follows twilight, as the case may be. It seems probable that the female watches all this from the deep cover, though I was not fortunate enough to glimpse her.

I often think how little we know of the wild creatures unless, as some of the wildlife biologists do, we spend years studying a single species and so train all our senses to capture the least significant detail. Even the trained woodsman or hunter, lacking scientific knowledge or the time for prolonged observation, can go far wrong in his conclusions. A theory long persisted that the mother woodcock, disturbed on her nest, would fly away with one of her young carried between her legs, and thus move all of them out of danger. There are so many reports of this that it cannot easily be dismissed as fiction, yet one observer flushed brooding females on more than four hundred occasions without ever seeing one carry off her young in this way.

Another misconception has developed about the number of broods raised annually by a pair of these birds. Most casual observers believe that in good seasons woodcock—and quail, too—will raise two broods, concluding this from the wide variance in size of young birds flushed both before and after the hunting season starts. What actually happens is that the adults, if their first nests are broken up, will nest again and again until they successfully bring off a brood. Once this has been done, they retire from the lists as parents for one season.

Wildlife Tribulations

Recently, as we were driving up through the central Ozarks on our way to Columbia, we witnessed a bizarre wildlife episode. Our road led at that point through a steeply rolling countryside where small farms and deserted fields are interspersed with more-extensive stretches of woodland. And we rounded a curve in one of these timbered areas just in time to see a hawk dive at some large dark object beside the highway embankment. The hawk took alarm at the approaching car and abandoned its pursuit to go soaring aloft, and at that moment a wild turkey gobbler ran out across the road.

The big bird was apparently uninjured, though somewhat confused, for it stopped at the fence and remained motionless for nearly a minute. Then it slipped through and moved slowly off across the open floor of the woodland. It was in plain sight for several moments at a distance of no more than a few yards, so that we had ample opportunity to observe it closely. It was taller and slimmer that its domestic cousin, with coppery-bronze feathers edged with black, which gave its plumage the effect of scales. And the legs were bright red instead of yellow, as in the tame turkey. We watched as long as it was in sight, then remained a moment longer to make sure the Cooper's hawk did not come back, though the gobbler was probably safe enough once it had gained the shelter of the forest.

I have speculated on what success the hawk might have had in attacking a bird two or three times as large as itself and several times as heavy. Yet the Cooper's hawk is one of the Accipiters; it dives like a miniature thunderbolt and lives entirely on live game. Its favorite habit is not soaring, like the big broad-winged hawks, which we often see riding the summer air waves, and which are clumsy at attacking. Instead, it likes to sit hidden in a tree in some likely spot, perhaps close to a poultry yard, then dash out at its victim and away before one even knows it is there. Though it is much smaller than the goshawk or the falcons, it can carry a large rabbit, chicken, or squirrel.

We left again for home before noon, richer by a beautiful eighteen-pound ham cured and smoked by Willard Woodson of Middletown. On the way out of Columbia we stopped for a visit with Tom Morelock at the University of Missouri, to make arrangements for another talk next week at the School of Journalism's annual Journalism Week. Then we spent a half hour walking through the Sanborn Field, one of the oldest and most famous agricultural experimental plots in the country, which has been in operation since 1883. Our arrival at home that evening confirmed our fears that the ice, snow, and freezing weather of the previous week end had put an end to our hopes for a bumper fruit crop this summer. Blossoms were black on the big Queen Anne cherry and the pie-cherry trees. The apples had just started to open and the earliest blossoms were gone. Now the later ones have opened, though we doubt that they will make fruit. Growth on the multiflora roses froze back and even the oats, rye, and other small grains were damaged to some extent. Worst of all, though this had happened before we left, a new calf, born out in the fields during the night of the storm, had either drowned or frozen before we could get to it next morning.

may

Lushness After Rain

Five consecutive days of rain—"falling like a gentle dew from heaven"—is something we haven't seen in the Ozarks during several years of severe drought. Moreover,—and this is something else we seldom see,—almost every drop has soaked into the ground. The showers fell gently and were spaced widely enough apart to let the earth take up the moisture. Just once the creek flushed up, rising perhaps a foot and turning muddy for a few hours, then dropping again to normal.

After such a spell of weather, woods and fields take on the luxuriant lushness of a tropical jungle. Pastures that had already begun to suffer from dry weather take a new lease on life and the lespedeza crop, which makes some of our finest midsummer grazing in normal years, is coming on apace. Trees and shrubs of every kind push out new shoots, while seedlings get a strong foothold for the future. Vegetable gardens, though you cannot get into them to hoe the weeds, show by far the best prospects we have seen in four springs. This brings country living back more closely to normal, with some assurance that peas, corn, beans, beets, onions, squash, cucumbers, and other garden produce will flow into the farm kitchen all summer with a surplus for freezing and canning.

At least once during each of the rainy days, we have pulled on boots and raincoats to make a round of the fields and check the cattle, and each time we get soaked. Finally at the week's end the clouds broke away and a misty sun shone through. As

soon as the morning chores were finished we took the binoculars, loaded Mike and Tiger into the car, and headed for the bottom fields, where we hadn't seen the cows with spring calves for a couple of days. Also we wanted to look at the ponds, which are now full to the brim, and to see how the new diversion terrace that we built to carry water to the Big Pond is functioning.

Because the fields were soft and wet, we parked at the northeast corner of the farm and hiked from there. Tiger flushed a pair of bobwhites from cover along the edge of the small wet-weather branch that runs through the field. We are delighted with the number of pairs of quail that we see, for it seems to indicate that the drought has not been as hard on them as we feared and that the self-imposed closed season which was observed by almost everyone in our valley last year helped boost the survival rate. Now the nesting season is just well started and we will hope that the hatch is successful and brings the quail population back to something like normal this year. Certainly cover conditions, as well as the food supply, should be better than in the last five years.

We found the cattle grazing contentedly in the woods pasture, then walked over to see how the oats were growing and decided they should make a bumper hay crop with all this early moisture. On the way back past the ponds, we kept a sharp eye out for birds. The first rather unusual one was a lone American egret, perched on the topmost branch of an ash tree beside the little Woods Pond.

When we came back to the house, we looked for a place to hang an unusually handsome long-necked South American gourd that Oscar Thalinger had fashioned into a birdhouse and brought to us. But every place we chose seemed already occupied. There were cardinals in the honeysuckle on the front porch, orchard orioles in the apple tree, bluebirds along the fence, a summer tanager in the sugar maple, a phoebe in the buckthorn above the machine-shop window, and wrens all over the place. Finally we found a suitable location in the peach tree and fully expect, even though most of the wrens have nested, that it will soon be occupied.

We are not quite sure about the nesting schedules of songbirds, though they seem to go ahead regardless of weather. One pair of bluebirds in a box on the back fence have brought off their first brood and are at the endless task of feeding the young. This nest is half hidden behind a hazlenut bush where the birds generally stop before carrying food into the box, and on sunny afternoons Mike likes to lie just at the foot of the bush. This puts both parents into a dither, but they soon decide the old red setter means no harm. And once they have made up their minds to this, the feeding process goes ahead steadily, as though Mike were far away.

Another pair that have brought off a brood are the Carolina wrens in the machine shed. As often happens with this species, the choice of a nesting site needlessly complicates the feeding operation, since food must be carried by a circuitous route: in through an adjoining shed, up through a crack in the eaves, and then down to the wall cabinet where the nest reposes precariously on its pile of nuts and bolts. Then there's a Bewick wren in the woodpile and another in a gourd, a phoebe over the stable door, more English sparrows than we like behind the shutters of the house, and doubtless many another.

Toward the end of May there finally arrive evenings when, the chores finished and supper eaten, it is warm enough to sit on the east terrace and wait for moonrise. On such evenings the lights of farmhouses over against the mountain twinkle through new foliage and a glow spreads gradually along the crest as the moment approaches for Diana to appear. The deepening dusk is filled with sounds of the spring night. From a far pasture the tinkle of Betsy's bell floats up to us. A calf bawls for its mother and is answered. The mockingbird bursts into song as if it were sunup, and we can hear the sleepy murmuring of bluebirds in their houses along the back fence.

We sit quiet, enjoying the night, and suddenly are aware of two sure signs of the approaching summer. Far down the valley a whippoorwill begins its ceaseless calling, and I say to Ginnie, in accordance with old-time Ozark tradition, that the time has come for her to start carrying in wood for the stove; from now on I'll be in the fields from daybreak until dark. And we think what a far cry that was from these days of tractors in the field and electric ranges in the farm kitchen, but agree that even in the old days we could not have been busier. As we talk, I suddenly see a wink of light just above the grass in the yard. Then there is another, and we realize the fireflies are back. There will be no more cold weather now and it will be safe to set out tomato plants in the garden.

Lessons in Nature

Every year at about this time I find myself thinking how much pleasure can be added to country living—or to city living, for that matter—by an interest in natural history. Life today is so full of gadgets and the many kinds of salesmanship which create a desire for these gadgets that we finally arrive at the point where we feel our very existence depends on them. The truth is, of course, that their existence depends on us. We become convinced that life would hardly be possible without the motors, radios, grocery stores, beauty shops, gasoline stations, and the manufacturers of a thousand articles that are always at our fingertips. We forget that, pleasant and useful and convenient as these things are, they are no more than services that we support. And in the final analysis, both they and we are altogether dependent upon certain very basic earth relationships. Today, as when the first sentient man walked upon earth, it is the same energy from the same sun, carried up to us through the food chains of the soil-water-plant-animal cycle, which makes human life possible.

Even we who live on the land, now that we have become

production specialists with lockers, refrigerators, and deep-freezes, are prone to forget where our food comes from. We roar across our fields on the seat of the tractor with our heads enveloped in exhaust fumes. No longer do we walk in the furrow with the sun on our backs, conscious of each plant the plow turns under, of the rich life that exists in good soil, of the blackbird following along behind us to pick up his morning meal. If we don't watch out, we are apt to find ourselves believing that it is the noise of our passage which makes the corn grow; and this is a conceit in which farming loses its real meaning.

It is impossible for the man or woman with an interest in natural history to fall into such errors as these. Such a person, be he countryman or bank teller, has a firm grasp upon the realities of life. He need not be a scientist, a trained botanist, ornithologist, or agricultural expert to develop that perception which gives meaning to the wonders of nature. He needs only curiosity and a keen eye. The bird life in a city park, the weedy growth on a vacant lot, the earthworms in a garden, the plant and animal life processes in a cow pasture—all of these have meaning. In all of them we may study the means by which nature achieves her ends of form and existence. Thus it is that an occasional farmer, though not nearly enough farmers, can contribute as much to agricultural science as the most-skilled technician working in the laboratory.

There are no limits set for the amateur naturalist; fascinating fields for study lie no farther away than one's own dooryard. Nor do I mean by this a mere re-cataloguing or verification of fact already established by professional authority, for in the whole area of the natural sciences are a thousand fields that have barely been glimpsed through gates that some amateur may swing wide open.

Most of the wildflowers that we write about each spring

grow out in the woodland along the limestone bluff above our creek. There are perhaps four hundred kinds of them, from March until frost, growing in constant succession or in direct competition. There are, in addition, perhaps a hundred species of shrubs and forty kinds of trees. Here is, obviously, the type of life community toward which nature builds when man does not interfere. The animal life in this area is as rich as the plant life and consists of many kinds of songbirds, rabbits, squirrels, foxes, raccoon, opossum—not to mention the insects, small rodents, and reptiles such as frogs, lizards, skinks, turtles, and snakes. Deer browse the area from time to time and now and then we permit a small amount of carefully managed grazing. There is a thick layer of humus on the ground, rich and moist and filled with a hundred life forms too small for the eye to see.

Here is the life cycle at its best. Here is a "biotic community" created by nature to make maximum use of organic and inorganic materials from the soil and of the energy of the sun to support a rich and complex life structure. Might not a farmer draw some interesting conclusions from such a landscape? Not far away from this woodland are many examples of how man uses the land with an almost absolute lack of comprehension of its life-producing potential. Here is a field planted to wheat, as it has been for many years past. It was plowed up and down the hill, sowed up and down the hill. Last winter the drill rows turned to small gullies which joined to make larger gullies. How many tons of the thin remaining topsoil left that field to go down the creek, I would not venture to say. Certainly there is no richness of humus here, nor of life within the soil.

A sense of real husbandry has as yet been grasped by far too few Americans, and this is something that goes beyond the crop we produce. We must develop a perceptive faculty to read the lessons of nature. When we do this, the whole vast accumulation of knowledge that is science takes on new meaning and we begin to understand the world we live in.

Farming Curiosities

The other day a neighbor stopped by to look at a buck rake we have for sale and we fell to talking about this strange and fascinating business of farming. He was experimenting with the new ladino clover that is just making a start in our country, and spoke of his wife's somewhat caustic comment when he appeared with a small sack containing twenty pounds of seed and admitted that it had cost forty dollars. "But you know how it gets hold of a fellow," he said, "this business of planting some new kind of seed and then watching for it to grow."

A farmer must have this feeling for the land bred in his bones. He must like his animals, too, if he is going to succeed with them. One of the most successful poultrymen I have ever known was showing me through his laying houses one day when I spotted an old rocking chair. We had seen a number of interesting pieces of improvised equipment on this farm, but I never knew a hen that preferred a rocking chair and said as much. My friend explained that whenever he had a half hour to spare, he came out and sat in this chair and watched the hens. He did this often, and there is little doubt that the intimate knowledge gained in this manner had much to do with his success. He had found, among other things, that certain hens which were potentially high producers were also very timid. Other hens crowded them away from the feeders. So he had invented a feeder that gave every hen an equal chance, and the egg production went up. The rocking-chair technique paid off.

One would hardly think that there would be much individuality in a herd of a hundred beef cattle, which look pretty much alike to begin with and are out on pasture a good part of the year. Yet there is. A good cattleman soon comes to know each head of stock, whether it is an easy keeper, a good mother, a heavy milker, a fence jumper. We have just been through one of those experiences that mean little to some farmers and a lot to some others. A cow took sick. Very often, when this happens, she will mope for a day or two and then turn up her toes with no effort whatever to keep on living. Sheep are even worse on this score than cows. But we doctored the old girl and she did everything she could to help us. Dr. Sheets came regularly each week, and we fed her glucose and tried every treatment we could think of.

As with a lot of seriously sick patients, one day she'd be better and the next day worse. Now and then she would try to eat, but mostly what food we got down her we poured down. That meant mixing and straining and feeding two or three quarts of gruel four or five times a day. Once or twice the old cow managed a bit of grass or we would see her chewing her cud. Never once did her ears droop, the sure sign of a losing battle with a sick cow. She was a game one, and Matt and Ginnie and I grew increasingly fond of her. We hated to lose her, moreover, for she was carrying a June calf. But finally, she knew she couldn't make it and we knew it, too. An animal has this sense of mortality, like some old settler when he asks "the women" to straighten the quilts and, turning his face to the wall, makes ready for the end. I have seen it happen enough times to make one wonder whether "dumb brute" is a good description for an animal. At any rate, I believe you have to like animals to do well with them.

It is interesting to see how the season pushes ahead regardless of weather. Now the last of the buckeye trees are in bloom and the bees seem to prefer these blossoms to any other. Only the grass is slow, so that we must shift the cattle from one pasture to another to keep it from being eaten down too close. But during the past week, the comeback has been fast.

Last week Matt and I tackled a job that I had been dreading for three years, and we find it not too bad. We have a forty-acre pasture, over on the east side of the farm, which is overgrown with hickory sprouts. Big fellows they are, and tough, for they had not been cut out in sixteen years before we came here. But we cleared and mowed a couple of acres last autumn and the bluegrass came up thick and green this spring, so we decided to tackle at least another strip. Brush clearing is a chore that once was turned over to some old fellow in the neighborhood who liked to work alone at a job where he was not pushed, and he demanded a modest wage accordingly. Today most farmers turn pale at the sight of a double-bitted ax and tackle the brush clearing with 2-4-5T or similar chemicals. But sixteen-year-old sprouts take a long time to die and a lot of spray equipment, and farming is a business where you frequently find yourself substituting muscle for machinery.

To date we have cleared probably eight acres, piled the brush, disked the cleared land, and fertilized it. If corn planting and haying do not overtake us, we hope to finish the job before hot weather. It is not easy work, but it is good work, and, as Matt puts it, "a fellow sure appreciates his beans" after a day of cutting brush.

You have a chance to observe a lot of things at a task like this. The steers come grazing past and you get them well sorted out in your mind as to quality. Here are the "good doers," as the cattlemen say, and here the ones that are cut too high in the flank and will have a hard time grading "good" at the market. We see the ducks come in to the pond and the band of a dozen jacksnipe that frequent the marshy land. There have been greater and lesser yellowlegs and a half-dozen kinds of sandpipers, and a pair of great blue herons work back and forth along the creek. The quail have paired off and there seem to be more of them than last season, with plenty of cover in which to raise their broods. A pair of sora rails have nested for the past three years at the Big Pond and we have seen the young ones, now almost full grown.

Now and then when we are both well winded, Matt and I walk over to see how the oats are coming along, or the bicolor lespedeza that we planted in the wildlife area. The preacher from Caledonia comes to fish for perch in the pond and pulls out several bluegills and a good bass while we watch with a twinge of envy.

Fishing on a May Evening

In these days of artificial lakes and ponds where the fishing season is open year round, there is no real reason for the enthusiastic angler ever to lay away his tackle. And this has many advantages. When tackle is in use from January to December, there is little chance for the oil in the reel to get gummy, or for a line that was put away wet to dry-rot and break just when you are tied into a good fish. The fly rod that is in constant action may develop a crook in its back from hard use, but it won't be stored away for months in a steam-heated room where its ferrules will become loose.

Winter fishing, however, is not my dish—unless it can be done in southern waters. In fact, I expect one reason my joints are stiff and practically refuse to unfold on frosty mornings is because, in my youth, I spent too many early spring days wading the icy waters of Ozark trout streams. There comes an evening along in early May when it is necessary to get out the fly rods, check the ferrules and wrappings, and otherwise make sure they are ready for the summer's work. Once they are in order, I lay out the tackle box and creel to see what is needed in the way of fresh equipment. Lines are stripped from the reels to make certain the enamel coating is still smooth so it will run easily through the guides. Flies, spinners, leaders, pork rind, and split shot all come in for their share of attention.

Once everything is ready I sneak off to the creek some evening along about five o'clock to find out whether the pan fish are striking. If they are, a half-dozen of the largest will find

their way into the creel, where a bed of watercress awaits them, while their lesser cousins are returned to the stream to grow for another season. Even if the fish are not striking, it is a wonderful time of year and a wonderful time of day to be wading a small Ozark stream.

The gear for this sort of fishing is a light fly rod with level line and a three-pound-test nylon leader some six feet long. It may take a few dozen casts to hit upon exactly the right lure, but it is safe enough to start out with a small Black Gnat or McGinty behind a No. 1 spinner and with about an inch of split pork rind dangling from the hook. If this does not attract the quarry, one can try everything else in the book;

although I have known good fly fishermen who claim that if this combination does not catch fish, one might as well go home. But who ever heard of going home because the fish were not striking, or of going fly fishing for pan fish on a May evening just to catch a certain number of pounds of fish?

Despite the predictions of some experts, I find that fishing in the little creeks has been badly hurt by the years of drought and low water. It is probably true, as claimed, that the hatching seasons were good because there were no flash floods to wash out the nesting beds or carry away the young fry. On the other hand, many creeks with gravel beds dried up to the point where only the pools remained. Thus thousands of small fish were lost in the shallows, while the concentrations of fish in the few remaining deep spots were easy prey for fishermen and all the small predators that must make their living along the streams. These creeks are still low, despite one spring rain; and unless there is a lot of precipitation in the next few weeks, we may see conditions even worse than during the past two summers.

There are, on the other hand, compensations for the low water levels and lack of floods. Increased vegetative growth within the stream itself helps furnish food for the minnows and fry, as well as for smaller organisms on which they feed. And along the gravelly banks a protective cover of willow and sycamore is starting, which, given another season, will help slow down the rush of future rises when they come.

There are always things to see along our creek on a May evening. Doves take off from the banks where they have come to pick up the gravel that helps grind their food. Young fox squirrels caught playing along the high banks go scurrying to the safety of their den trees. In one deep pool I glimpse the sleek form of a muskrat just as it disappears into a tangle of roots. Out over the valley, nighthawks wheel in their evening hunt for insects. A blue grosbeak, rare in our valley, warbles from a fencepost beside the meadow, and a tiny blue-gray gnatcatcher scolds from a branch so close overhead that I can almost touch it. Indigo buntings flash in the late sunlight and a catbird sings from the thicket.

All of these I see with one eye as I gauge the distance into each pocket and swirl of the stream where the green perch may be lurking, and at the same time try to make sure that my back cast does not become entangled in a treetop. Dusk falls in the valley and I count a half-dozen fish in the creel—enough for breakfast. And when I climb the steep path to the top of the bluff and head for home, I am surprised to find that up on the high ground the sun is still shining.

Lively Adventures

Young Tiger Kilkelly, the Irish setter pup, is a source of constant entertainment. Often I have heard it said that the big red Irishmen are hardheaded, capricious, and difficult to train; that they seldom make a bird dog until they are four years old; and that in breeding them for bench and show, breeders have largely killed their noses and hunting instinct. But this is not true of our old Mike and, from all the signs, it isn't going to be true of the young dog. He grows like a weed and, from all I know of the Irish-setter type, is developing into a fine animal. He is fast as a greyhound and seems to have natural nose and hunting instinct. He takes to water like a duck and retrieves everything from butterflies, which he catches on the wing, to rubber boots that are carelessly left within his reach. He is as full of energy and enthusiasm as a boy just out of school, yet learns to mind in a remarkably short time.

When our grandson Ricky was visiting recently, he and I noticed the pup lying out in the yard gazing intently at some small object between his front paws, which he made no attempt to touch. Suddenly the object moved and Tiger jumped a foot in the air in surprise, then immediately lay down with the thing between his paws and his nose an inch or two away. At first we thought it must be a garden toad; then we heard a wren fussing on the fence close by. I called to the pup and he came to me, although reluctantly. Leaving him for Ricky to hold, I went and picked up a baby wren—entirely untouched and un-harmed—and deposited it in a nearby brush pile. After that, we hiked out to the field to see some calves, and Tiger went along willingly. But an hour later, when we had forgotten the in-cident, we discovered the pup lying out beside the brush pile, gazing intently into it. He had found the baby wren again, though now it was safely out of reach and almost ready to fly.

Down in the bottom fields near the Big Pond, some weeks ago, we discovered a young blue goose grazing with the cattle. Evidently injured, so that it cannot fly, it can run like a streak and thus far has been able to avoid ending up as a meal for a fox. On one occasion, when I was working nearby in the field, I saw Tiger swimming round and round in the pond after the goose. It was an unequal contest, for whenever the pup came too near, the bird would dive. Then Tiger would tread water, turning his head in every direction until the goose appeared again; whereupon the pup would go after it again until I was afraid he would drown from exhaustion. We hur-ried to the pond and called Tiger, who at once gave up the pursuit and swam over to us. But on one other occasion, when he discovered the goose on a much smaller pond in a clump of trees, he caught it and held on without hurting it, then let it go and came to me when I called.

The box tortoises that wander the fields and woods in large numbers at this season seem to intrigue the bird-dog pup. One day, when I was working in this same field, I saw Tiger head-ing for the little pond with some large object in his mouth. He waded out neck-deep and dropped it, then went back to ranging the field. Next time I looked, he was heading for the pond again and went through the same performance. The third time this happened I climbed down from the tractor and hurried over to see what it was all about. Tiger came carrying a huge box tortoise. He waded out into the pond, opened his mouth, dropped the tortoise into the water, and headed for the field again. Fortunately for the tortoise, it can swim—or at least float.

Tiger occasionally provides a good laugh by flushing a cottontail, starting after it like a streak of lightning and then running right over the rabbit without ever seeing it. Yards farther on he will suddenly realize that there is no longer any rabbit scent in his nose and circle back to start over again. Once or twice I have seen him actually catch his rabbit, which startled him so that he at once let go of it; whereupon the quarry picks itself up and makes for the safety of the nearest brush pile or groundhog burrow.

Now and then I read about fishing dogs, and I have no doubt that with a little training Tiger could be taught to retrieve fish. Every time we are near the creek, he goes fishing. His favorite method is to corner a bunch of minnows in the shallow water at the head of a riffle—and then he goes nearly wild with excitement. He tries to step on them or to catch them in his mouth, often tumbling head over heels and getting a good ducking for his efforts. And he will keep this up for a half hour at a time, never discouraged by the fact that so far he has not caught a fish.

Living with the Country

This is not only the year of the seventeen-year cicada, "locust," but also of the little brown May beetle that buzzes about the lights at night and is often miscalled "June bug." Early on Sunday morning, as I was milking, a car horn tooted in the driveway and I went out to find our mailman and good friend John Akers. John is a great outdoorsman with a surprising amount of knowledge about how many bobwhites are nesting along his country route, where the foxes have their dens, how the raccoon crop is making out, and even in what areas the illegal deer kill is heaviest. He also has a natural curiosity about every kind of bird, animal, and insect, and in his spare time is an excellent beekeeper.

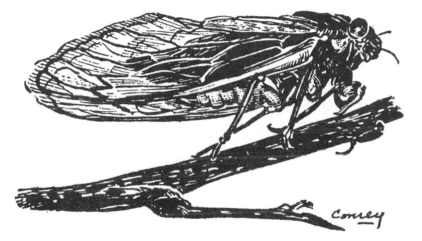

From time to time John reports some unusual occurrence in the world of the outdoors. This morning he called us over to his car, opened the trunk, and displayed two big five-gallon buckets full of May beetles. All of these had been captured by placing a large tub of water under one light in his back yard, and since then he has reported heavy damage to many trees, especially the oaks, along his route. The May beetle, or some other insect, is cutting the leaves and practically stripping the trees. Evidently the insects are not evenly distributed, because here at Possum Trot we have no more than the normal number.

May beetles belong to the family of scarabs, of which the June bug or figeater is an even better-known variety, the former being a plain dull brown and the latter a handsome green. May beetle larvae are the big white grubs often turned up in garden soil and sometimes used as bait for such small pan fish as bluegill. They feed on the roots of grass ordinarily, but also like roots of young conifers or of anything planted on newly turned sod. The adults, when they hatch, come up out of the ground. At night they feed on the leaves of many deciduous trees, so that in seasons of a big hatch they can do considerable harm. In daytime they stay hidden in the grass.

When you live in the country you have to learn to get along with it. Maybe you don't like snakes or toads or lizards or chiggers or ticks, but you have to take them in your stride. And since we tend to subscribe to the Schweitzerian philosophy of "reverence for life," we don't kill even a snake unless it is poisonous or is obviously destroying our songbirds. We know most snakes are harmless, many are useful, and all of them are part of living in the country. For the one poisonous species, the copperhead, we keep a sharp eye out.

Chiggers and ticks are not insects, but belong to the class of Arachnids, along with the spiders, scorpions, and daddy longlegs or harvestmen. There has evidently been quite a build-up of these pests due to the long series of dry and comparatively mild winters, which assures a high rate of survival. Ticks come in about three sizes and, I am told, must attach themselves to a host such as a squirrel, rabbit, dog, cow, or human and then feed in order to reproduce. When land is heavily pastured over a period of years, it is apt to become badly infested. Dipping or spraying helps control these pests on cattle. Our dogs are constantly in the water and wash off any repellent we put on them, so must be kept outdoors and gone over carefully each day. As for ourselves, we can use repellents, but ticks get on our clothing anyway and all we can do is try not to bring them into the house with us. When we remember it, chiggers can be controlled easily by dusting thoroughly with sulphur.

Garden insects continue to thrive, despite poisons. Last evening, after setting out tomatoes, peppers, and eggplant fresh from the nursery, I went to the garden before dark to have a final look at my handiwork. The eggplants looked sick and examination showed them to be literally weighted down with tiny black hopping insects. As quickly as possible I dusted them with a bug powder; the tiny bugs took off and this morning the plants had revived. How many times we will have to repeat this to produce eggplants is yet to be answered.

The blister beetle is another of our worst garden pests, a tremendous eater and sometimes appearing in such numbers as to do great damage before it can be brought under control. One of its favorite foods is the foliage of the clematis, and I have seen the blister beetles, in a single day, defoliate completely a clematis vine covering an area of perhaps 120 square feet. The fact that the beetles seem to arrive in armies of hundreds or even thousands led me to check their life history, and the wonder is that these insects are able to survive at all. Blister beetles belong to the family Meloidae, a fairly numerous tribe. The ones we see most often in the garden are obnoxious-looking creatures of dull black or gray and black with rather heavy wings. They are about three fourths of an inch in length with a cylindrical body and a big abdomen generally swollen from eating our vegetables. The larvae are either predacious or parisitic on the eggs of one of the mason bees or flower bees of the family Apidae.

There are at least six known larval stages of the blister beetle; the first one is a tiny insect with large jaws, long legs for grasping, and, at the back of its body, a sort of adhesive pad that enables it to stand on its tail. When this larva hatches, it climbs up onto a flower blossom and waits for some flying insect to come by. This in itself seems an unlikely chance, and even if the infant *Meloe* is successful in grasping a passing insect, the percentage in favor of that being a mason bee would appear infinitesimally small. If it attaches itself to the wrong insect, it perishes in the course of its free ride; and of course, the vast majority of the larvae must die without ever encountering a flying insect of any kind.

When the one-in-a-million chance comes along and the *Meloe* hitchhikes home with the mason bee, it must wait until the bee lays an egg in a drop of honey, then transfer itself from the bee to the egg, which it begins eating. Just before the egg is completely consumed, the *Meloe* must be transformed into a second larval form that will not drown in the surrounding honey. Yet even this is simply another step in the development of the adult blister beetle, since it must go through three or four more larval stages before reaching maturity. And as I go out to spray the blister beetles in the garden, these propositions occur to me: how remarkable that enough larvae of the Meloidae manage to complete their life cycle so that they can attack my potato patch in seemingly countless thousands. And why did Nature ever devise such a complex and altogether improbable scheme to enable the repulsive blister beetle to survive?

No doubt we have brought many of these garden pests on ourselves, simply through overcultivation. And we have seen evidence that when ground is fertile enough, packed with organic matter and with every mineral and trace element needed for perfect plant growth, either there are fewer bugs or the plants are so strong that the insects have no effect on them. Despite many loads of manure and plenty of lime and fertilizer, we have not reached the optimum in garden soils. But we keep trying.

SUMMER

june

Ripening Grain

Out from our west porch, which looks toward the sunset, a field of ripening grain rises in a gentle swell that at its highest point shuts out the distant horizon. The surface of the field is like the surface of the ocean, endlessly in motion. Sometimes, when there is a strong, steady wind, it rises and falls in waves that bend the tall stems almost to the ground. And sometimes a vagrant breeze sets the small ripples to chasing each other across the nodding heads. Only when the wind dies completely, as happens sometimes at sunrise and sunset, is the surface of the field at rest.

We are likely to look at such a field and say, "It has been a fine season for oats," without giving a second thought to the complex life structure that this bit of land supports. Hidden deep down beneath the stems of the grain is a thick stand of new grasses and clover, seeded there to furnish next summer's hay and pasture. Rabbits have made their nests in the field and come out in the late evening to play in the yard. Old Mike, half dozing, watches them without moving, though he follows them with nose and eyes. He seldom gives chase, for he learned long ago that he never catches a cottontail.

In early morning and late evening the bobwhites call from

the fencerows. And when Tiger, the pup, goes bouncing through the grain, we realize how many more birds use the field for cover. There are the prairie horned larks, small ground-loving birds that seldom perch on anything higher than a clod of earth. They start hurriedly from the field with soft, chattering whistled notes and almost always circle back to their starting point after a short flight, making fine sport for a pup who likes to chase everything in sight. The prairie and northern horned larks are the only true American members of the family best represented in Europe and Britain by the skylark. And like their European cousins, the horned larks during the mating season mount high into the air and sing as they go—a song that is not loud, yet echoes the wild, free spirit of the prairie.

I recall a story about the famous old scientist who was asked what he felt had been the most momentous discovery in the whole field of science during his lifetime. He replied that when he was a very young man, a cubic foot of earth was considered to contain something like a million of the little living creatures called bacteria. And now that he was an old man, he knew this cubic foot of earth contained many billion bacteria. To him, the most wonderful thing in his career had been the discovery of the almost infinite life-carrying capacity of this earth of ours.

Looking out across our field of grain, I believe that one of the things we learn from farming is that there are few short cuts and few certainties, at least in the affairs of men. Some things we know are inevitable, like the broad sweep of the seasons—the awakening of springtime, summer's growth, autumn with its harvest, and winter when the earth rests and renews its strength. Yet this is a cycle over which husbandmen have no control and to which we must shape our lives. Nor do we have much to say about the way the seasons run. Thus spring may be long and wet and cold, or it may pass in a handful of days and plunge at once into the heat of summer. In the same way, the grain we plant has been carefully selected and bred through many centuries for the best yield. Yet we must still plow and prepare the ground, plant the seed, then wait for rain and sun to cause the plant to grow and ripen for the harvest.

Eyes That Cannot See

A fellow I once met boasted that he had loaded his family into the car and driven through forty-seven states in exactly forty-eight days. The kids replenished their comic books at every stop, his wife studied the road maps as they drove along, and he kept his eyes glued to the highway. I questioned him about some of the beauty of the state in which he lived and was rewarded with a blank stare. Not for him were the dogwood and redbud blooming along country roads in April, the golden crops of June mellowing toward harvest, the skein of geese traversing the October sky. His interest was all in going, and not at all in where he was going or what might be seen along the way.

I thought of this traveler this morning as I drove the tractor down to Joe Rickett's farm to return the cultivator we had borrowed the day before. The sun wasn't long above the mountain and the heat of the June day was still an hour or so away. For the first half mile I rolled along the old county road that runs down to the creek and then up past the Sutton place and on to Harry Russell's where it joins again with the highway.

Out in the Nickelson's alfalfa field a pair of young groundhogs were busily gathering their breakfast, not at all disturbed by the clatter of my motor. Bobwhites whistled from fencerows and soon I disturbed a pair that have their nest in the cover at the edge of our cornfield. For two hundred yards they trotted down the dusty road ahead of me, performing the age-old ritual of leading an enemy away from their nest, then whirred off into the woods. It would be hard to say, unless one had a summer of leisure for the study, how many pairs of birds nest in these thickets of pawpaw, wild grape, buckthorn, horse chestnut, and in the hedges of multiflora rose.

Where the road swings south to flank the creek, the tractor motor disturbed our kingfisher from his hunting perch on the cable that holds the water gap; and as he took off with a loud rattle, he started up the little green heron—"fly up the creek," we used to call him when we were youngsters—which flew off with a harsh alarm note. At the mailboxes a fox squirrel with undulating tail ambled across the road and climbed the big burr-oak tree.

Up the steep hill toward the Sutton place, a pair of cotton-tails moved just far enough off into the cover to let me go past and a pair of Carolina wrens scolded from the fencerow. Otho Sutton was plowing out his garden at the top of the hill, and we stopped to pass the time of day while a mocking bird sang from the top of a telephone pole, the highest handy perch. Up across the field toward the Stricklins, I could see Ern greasing the big red baler, getting ready for the day's work in the hay fields, and recalled that on the way back I must stop to talk with him about our next mqwing. There were meadowlarks singing from the field and a pair of handsome kingbirds darted out from the fence posts in pursuit of insects. "Bee martin" is the name by which they are known to most country folk, though careful investigation shows that their food consists almost entirely of plant-eating insects. A more appropriate name, as anyone will agree who has seen the intrepid kingbird attacking a robber crow or hawk, is the Latin designation, *Tyrannus tyrannus*.

A spring branch runs down through Harry Russell's pasture and here a pair of killdeer evidently have their nest, for the birds take alarm at the approach of the tractor. The mother bird puts on a great show of limping off with a trailing wing while the male circles above me, calling ceaselessly. I found Harry taking advantage of the morning coolness to hoe out his potato patch and stopped to see whether Ethel, his wife, could come over to help Ginnie get her peas ready for the freezer and whether Matt and I can come help put up his baled oats, as he worked with us when we put ours in the barn last Saturday.

Next stop was at the Hubert Russells, where he and Lawrence and Bob were getting ready to head for the alfalfa field. Bob is going to bring his combine up next week to harvest our field of barley, but they are waiting for the arrival of a new sickle bar and are not quite sure when it will get here. There is a saying about cutting grain with the combine, however, which gives us comfort at the delay. "Whenever you figure your grain is ready for the combine," it runs, "just take off a week and go fishing. Then go home and go to work cutting it." The dryer the crop, the better it will work, so long as the straw has not started to break down.

At the Ricketts' house, the whole family was assembled for the day's chores. Fannie and Lorraine and Jessie, along with the youngsters, were out in the garden, pulling pea vines and stripping the peas into baskets for canning and freezing. Joe and Junior and Johnnie, along with Henry Campbell and Chris Poston, were making ready the combine for a day in the wheatfields. I unhooked the cultivator and thanked them for the loan, then started up the highway for home and our own haying. It wasn't a long journey—not more than a mile or two—yet I wish my acquaintance, the cross-country motorist, might discover that the true pleasure in traveling lies in what we see along the way.

All Nature Sings

Although weather creates constant problems for the farmer, few of these are without some compensation. The shower that delays the haying is the same one that causes the corn to shoot up overnight and keeps the pastures green. Even on the mown hayfields you can fairly see the clover and alfalfa sending out new shoots, while the young grasses stool out and push forth green leaves. When you walk out across the land in the evening after the shower, there is the rich smell of moist earth and growing things, as when you are in a greenhouse. Even though the days start early and end at dark, as far as work is concerned,

there is constant satisfaction in observing the richness of the fields. Here is land that produced, ten years ago when we came here, perhaps eight bushels of wheat to the acre. Today the first cutting of brome grass, alfalfa, and red clover runs well over two tons, or a total of five tons for the season. Translated into terms of beef, which is the end product at Possum Trot Farm, this means that land which was producing a scant hundred pounds per acre when we came here is today capable of turning out five hundred pounds of beef of better quality.

There is no miracle about this. It is a matter of time, hard work, and a willingness to sacrifice immediate gain for the ultimate good of the land. It is a matter of studying constantly the ways in which nature manages to produce the endless and almost profligate richness of her landscape and, in so far as is possible, using these methods for man's purposes. That the thing works is becoming constantly more obvious as time goes on. That it is done so little is one of the great tragedies of farming the world over.

As the fertility of the soil and the richness of the flora increase, so does our population of wildlife. After breakfast on a recent morning, we stole an hour to walk out along the bluff above the creek to see what new wildflowers were in bloom, and learned again a lesson that we know all too well. This is that in order to observe the whole wonderful flora of a Missouri spring and summer, even on a few acres such as our woodland embraces, one must never let a week go by without a careful check-up. Our most exciting discovery on this walk was of a great bed of wild blue iris in full bloom, a bed that we had often observed earlier in the spring and set down as being the blackberry lily. There is a bed of these latter growing nearby; and because we had never visited this particular spot during the second week in June, we had missed this beautiful sight. We found several clumps of the common beardtongue, or penstemon, growing five feet tall and with flowers as handsome as any one might find in the garden. Wild petunias are in bloom and the limestone glades are covered with pennyroyal in full blossom.

The tall meadow rue, which grows to a height of five feet in the rich limestone soil, shows great clusters of tiny flowers, and the wild hydrangea along the overhanging bluffs is budding. Climbing milkweed, wild clematis, and smilax are interesting vines that put forth their blossoms at this season, and of these the milkweed is perhaps least known. Its broad, heart-shaped leaves somewhat resemble the leaves of a climbing bean, and where each pair of leaves branch out from the stem are clusters of handsome brownish purple flowers.

The interesting thing about such a bit of wild land, especially where the soil is of a limestone base and there is plenty of humus built up by leaf mold, is the truly amazing complexity of the growth. Now the plants of early spring have entirely disappeared; bloodroot and many others that covered the ground with a thick growth. May apple and jack-in-the-pulpit and Solomon's seal can still be seen, but soon they will also disappear, except for the seed stalk of the jack-in-the-pulpit, which then becomes known as Indian turnip. Already this land is on the third or fourth complete succession of wild crops, with many fall-blooming varieties still to appear. Native grasses mix with the tame ones, wild legumes with clover, Korean lespedeza, and the tall lespedeza sericea, which we have broadcast to serve as wildlife cover and help in healing the gullies caused by long years of cattle grazing on the steep bluff.

New tree growth is equally interesting to observe. Thousands of young cedars are starting up on this natural cedar habitat. But with these are the redbuds by hundreds, as well as oaks of a dozen varieties, wild cherry, sugar maple, and many others. The growth of shrubs and briers is equally luxuriant. Here are a dozen hawthorns, woolly bumelia, spice bush, buckthorn, leatherwood, wahoo, bladdernut, pawpaw, hydrangea, to mention only a few. All of these grow in endless succession, in unbelievable profusion and confusion. Yet who can doubt that there is here an underlying harmony as well as countless necessary relationships? If there were not, then some species would certainly become dominant; yet it is clear to us that the exact opposite is true. Each year that we protect this land it grows richer in its ability to produce, more complex in the varieties that it produces.

Migrating with Man

"Regard the flowers at eventide as, one after the other, they close in the setting sun. Strange is the feeling that then presses in upon you—a feeling of enigmatic fear in the presence of this blind dreamlike earth-bound existence. The dumb forest, the silent meadows, this bush, that twig, do not stir themselves; it is the wind that plays with them. Only the little gnat is free— he dances still in the evening light, he moves whither he will."

Thus Oswald Spengler opened the second volume of his monumental *Decline of the West* to point the difference between the great divisions of living things—the plant and animal kingdoms. The individual plant is a part of the landscape, growing where chance makes it take root. It cannot will for itself or choose for itself. The animal can choose, and in this fact lies history. Only the animal meets danger with willed answer and challenge with response. As Spengler puts it, "The midget swarm that dances on and on, that solitary bird still flying through the evening, the fox approaching furtively the nest—these are little worlds of their own within another great world. An animalcule in a drop of water, too tiny to be perceived by the human eye, though it lasts but a second and has but a corner of this drop as its field—nevertheless is free and independent in the face of the universe. The giant oak, upon one of whose leaves the droplet hangs, is not."

In the face of this great law of nature—that the plant grows where chance makes it take root—there are members of the plant kingdom that are great travelers. This thought came to me only this evening as I attacked the weeds in our vegetable garden. My enemies there make up a formidable list, yet even more interesting is that almost every one of them is a plant that has followed man through countless centuries and across the entire face of the globe. Thus even our common pigweed,

Amaranthus retroflexus, is as old as human history. Wherever men have tilled the soil, there the amaranth has appeared. Its seed in prehistoric times was used for food, and during man's historic migrations the amaranth has migrated with him.

If I were to list by their Latin names the plants which fell beneath my newly sharpened hoe, there are some you might not recognize. *Abutilon theophrasti, Agrostemma githago, Arctium minus, Chenopodium alba, Cirsium arvense, Datura stramonium, Rumex crispus*—you would naturally take these to be foreigners and so they are. Put into more colloquial language, these are cottonweed, corn cockle, burdock, lamb's quarter, Canada thistle, Jimson weed, and curly dock—as fine a bunch of fertility stealers as one could put together. It isn't even easy to recall, in fact, many of our common weeds that are really natives of the Western Hemisphere, although two that come to mind are ragweed, with the inappropriate name of *Ambrosia,* and horse nettle, a member of the potato family scientifically known as *Solanum carolinense.*

This characteristic that plants have of following man is developed to a high degree. The Jimson weed, for example, must even carry along or develop in its new home a special kind of moth, the sphinx, to fertilize its flowers. The plant blooms at night, with a bell-shaped flower that has a funnellike tube for the corolla. And the sphinx moth, which hatches from the cocoon of the tomato worm, is a night-flying species with an especially long proboscis for reaching into the deep-belled flowers. This seems a lot of trouble to perpetuate a noxious weed that is poisonous to all domestic livestock as well as to human beings. The plant came by its American name in an interesting, though tragic, way. During a food shortage in early Jamestown, settlers who ate the datura became crazed, the symptoms of the alkaloid poison being loss of sight and co-ordination, convulsions, mania, and sometimes death. The

"Jimson" comes from Jamestown and the plant has been called the Jamestown lily, as well as devil's trumpet and mad apple. In the same way that plants travel with man, though not of their own volition, there are some that have a definite affinity for animals. One of our field weeds is croton, with the common name of hogwort. And wherever you find croton growing, you can be fairly certain that at some time in the past the area has been intensively pastured by pigs. There are also many plants, like the beggar's-tick trefoil and some of the cacti, that depend on animals to carry and distribute their seed, as well as water plants that travel on the legs or in the craws of wading birds.

In addition to plants that man transports involuntarily are those he deliberately moves from one place to another on the landscape. Here in the United States these include a large proportion of the species that make up our domestic crops: forage grasses, cereals, except corn (cereals are also grasses), and many legumes. A large number of domesticated flowering plants escape from gardens and establish themselves successfully in the wild, a good example being the blackberry lily, *Balamcanda chinensis,* which grows prolifically in the Ozark glades and actually belongs to the iris family. Other common introductions from foreign lands that have gone wild and acclimated themselves are bouncing Bet, periwinkle, scarlet pimpernel, day lily, and balsam apple. In his "Check List of the Flowering Plants of Missouri," Bill Bauer gives nearly three hundred species found here in the wild that had their origin in other lands.

Thus plants take over the far places of the earth. They cannot, like animals, respond to danger; when the grazing cow curls out her long tongue, the clover fulfills its destiny. And while the cottontail rabbit is generally successful in meeting the response to danger, reaching its brush pile a jump ahead of

Tiger, it still lives out its life within an area of an acre or two. Even the white-tailed deer, which is highly mobile and fleet of foot, will often travel its whole life over an area only a few miles square unless famine or fire or extraordinary danger drives it from its regular haunts.

Time to Think

Now and then—but not as often as I'd like, since leisure is a commodity that a farmer rarely comes by—I spend an evening with my old friend Henry David Thoreau. Our meeting ground is most often the doorstep of his cabin above Walden Pond, although with almost equal pleasure I occasionally accompany him as he floats peacefully down those little rivers of New England, the Concord and the Merrimack. The experience of such an evening is always satisfactory and salutary. As Sidney Alexander put it in reviewing Hough's biography of Thoreau: "More than ever we need this greatest nonconformist of all. As the refrigerators, Thunderbirds, TV sets and washing machines tumble forth from the cornucopia, someone must stand aside and whisper to us in a voice like a wind soughing through the tops of tall pines, 'Simplify, simplify, simplify.' And as new corporative man finds that his job has become a castle, inclosing his private life as well, more than ever we need to remember that there is always Henry strolling outside the walls, free."

I suppose this is the reason I enjoy these visits with the sage of Walden Pond: that he is constantly concerned, in a time of collectivism, with "man the individual" rather than "men in the mass." He is as thorny as a prickly ash, ready to scratch pretensions of every sort. Yet these thorns can scratch without breaking off and working their way deeper into the flesh, as do the thorns of some briers, as well as of some social philosophers.

There are many who make the mistake of assuming that Thoreau built his cabin in Ralph Waldo Emerson's woodlot because he was by nature a hermit or a recluse—or because he wished to prove something about the art of survival. Nothing could be farther from the case than this. It is true that he sought seclusion and simplicity, but I think that he wanted what few of us will ever have or pay the price to achieve: time and quiet and solitude to think out the real values of living. Nor did he intend to set a fashion of "taking to the woods." He makes this plain when he says, "I would not have anyone adopt my mode of living on any account; for, beside that before he has fairly learned it I may have found another for myself, I desire that there be as many different persons in the world as possible; but I would have each one be very careful to find out and pursue his own way, and not his father's or his mother's or his neighbor's instead."

We recently undertook to add a room to our house at Possum Trot, an enterprise that seemed simple enough in contemplation but became more complicated as it progressed. It is a modest-enough room, with a bath and an areaway leading to the kitchen, some sixteen by eighteen feet in size and all under one roof. Yet it has occupied a good share of our time this past three weeks, along with that of neighbor-carpenter Stan Turner, and is still a long way from completion. Rough lumber for the framing was sawed out at their mill by Reed and Russell. Nails and roofing came from Hixson's Store at Belleview. Iron County Lumber Company furnished doors and windows, hardware, trim, flooring, and other accessories. Russ Calvert came and roughed in the plumbing and will install the fixtures and wiring, while Emory Depew tapped onto the furnace and ran the heating ducts. Frank Tyndall applied two coats of paint to the exterior and is waiting word to come finish the inside and outside painting.

It is going to be an eminently satisfactory addition to the house. Yet I find myself envying my friend Thoreau, who once built for himself a whole house that was just about the size of this room. He borrowed an ax from a neighbor, who loaned it with some misgiving but got it back sharper than when he loaned it. With the ax a suitable number of young pines were felled in leisurely fashion, to hear Thoreau tell it, and hewn square for sills and framing. Most of the boards for siding and roof came from a railroad worker's shanty, purchased for the sum of $4.75 from the owner, who was moving away, and then dismantled and carted to the new building site. There were a few other oddments: old brick for the chimney, lime for mortar, two secondhand windows, nails, hinges, and a door latch. The total cash expenditure came to $28.12, by the builder's account, though this did not include his labor.

The building of Thoreau's cabin beside Walden Pond was, for all its simplicity, a rather jolly undertaking. After he had cut the logs and hewed the timbers and mortised the ends and laid the foundation stones, he invited his philosopher friends from Concord to the raising of the walls. But being a practical young man, he also had his farmer neighbor Edmund Hosmer on hand with his three sons to assure a workmanlike job. And this it turned out to be, for history has it that the cabin was twice moved, then at last incorporated into a barn, where its identity was finally lost. The whole occasion of the house-building was auspicious. It was springtime beside Walden Pond and "the oaks, hickories, maples and other trees, just putting out amidst the pine woods around the water, imparted a brightness like sunshine to the landscape."

Those who remember only Thoreau's chapter on "Solitude" miss the whole neighborliness of the Walden experiment. It began with the building of the cabin and continued during his entire "two years, two months and two days" of residence there. His beanfield fronted on the old road that ran from Lincoln to Concord, so that farmers stopped to pass the time of day and leave a bit of advice on how to fertilize a garden. Townsmen driving by in their shiny gigs were apt to look askance and with some misgiving at one who, so early in life, had taken the true measure of the value and handicaps of material possessions. Visitors came constantly to Thoreau's doorstep, some out of friendliness and some from curiosity. It is plain from his writing that his measure of a man was not the elegance of the conveyance that brought him there.

No one could have been less of a recluse than young Henry. Walden Pond was hardly a wilderness and few days passed without a journey to Concord. Sunday generally found Thoreau at family dinner with the Emersons, where the afternoons must have been spent in good talk. And on the way home, more often than not, he would stop to share with Farmer Hosmer that immemorial New England Sunday-night supper, the remains of Saturday's baked beans. As for company at his cabin, he says, "I had more visitors while I lived in the woods than at any other period in my life. Fewer came to see me upon trivial business. In this respect my company was winnowed by mere distance from town." Simple woodchopper, old fisherman, or Yankee seer, Thoreau's "two chairs for friendship and three for society" were often filled and life at Walden Pond was a life of neighborliness.

The book *Walden, or Life in the Woods* was a long time ripening, although the notes for it were doubtless set down during those leisurely months beside his pond. Thoreau began the actual writing in 1846, using the chapters as they developed for lectures before the Concord Lyceum, where his audience included such notables as his friend Emerson. For eight years the material was written and rewritten, revised and polished; and it was not until 1854 that the manuscript went off to the printer.

It is well enough to aim for the simple life, though few are willing to make the sacrifice in so-called comforts and possessions that is its inevitable price. Most of us, and we among them, are like Thoreau's farmer who, in order to get his shoestrings or other simple necessities, must speculate in herds of cattle. We set our traps with hairsprings to catch comfort and independence, and then get our own leg caught in them. And we forget that while civilization is improving our houses, albeit at heavy cost, it does a far poorer job of improving the human beings who inhabit them. Palaces, says Thoreau, are easier to create than noblemen.

Perhaps the most important thing about *Walden* is that it is a leisurely book, written out of the fullness of days and nights of contemplation. There was time to think, time to vegetate, time to drain the full meaning from each observation of the small wild creatures of his woodland. He became, indeed, a creature of that woodland as he floated at midnight over the pond's surface in his skiff or sat through long summer afternoons beside its shore, hearing the world's cares, like the church bells of Concord, come faintly on the soft wind, "a melody which the air had strained, and which had conversed with every leaf and needle of the wood."

We conformists of the world watch Thoreau with a touch of envy—a man who, like Thomas Jefferson, believed that Nature plus a decent respect for the opinions of mankind, without too much regard for religious sanctions or the vote of the majority, would settle most problems of human conduct. Small wonder that Tolstoy was a disciple of Thoreau and that Mahatma Gandhi acknowledged a deep debt to his writing.

Magic Hour

When evening comes, in the brief time between dusk and darkness, we like to walk out across the high ridge field beside the house. Along the hills that encircle our valley a purple haze has fallen, forerunner of the night. Far overhead a solitary hawk, late home from hunting and silhouetted sharp against the sky, heads for its nest on the Caledonia hill, or a great blue heron crosses with slow wingbeat to the pond.

This is the hour when swallows circle, rising and dipping to follow some hatch of insects; and the songbirds, stilled during the heat of the summer day, come again to life. The meadowlark gives its liquid call, a bobwhite whistles from a fence post, and then we hear the soft note of the field sparrow, a small silver bell ringing in the fencerow.

Down along the high fence of multiflora rose that borders the field we take our way, and whistle for Daisy and Ribbon.

They come up, sleek and fat as butterballs, for the apples they know Ginnie has brought along. Ribbon and Daisy seem content to graze and then share in the chores when we have cattle to move about the farm and saddle them up in earnest. Perhaps when the cool days of autumn come and the work is in hand, there will be time to ride for pleasure.

Farther along in the field our yearling heifers, grazing in a line, raise their white faces to watch us placidly. The grass is short and we study them carefully to make certain they are getting enough to eat. But their broad, flat backs and short, straight legs and well-filled flanks testify to the hard work we have put in on these fields since we came to Possum Trot ten years ago. There is nothing that gives us quite so much pleasure as cattle grazing a deep, lush pasture; even in this time of extreme drought it is plain that the revitalized land puts forth the nutrients for growth and health.

Darkness falls at last and we stand awhile to watch the first stars appear in the sky and the myriad fireflies flickering above the field. The evening is a benediction and we can forget, for a few moments, the tiredness of the day that is past and the tasks of the one that lies ahead. Even the terrible drought, which is bringing disaster to farmers throughout our part of the Ozark country, can be pushed aside in this moment as darkness hides the sere, brown grass and cracking earth. Tomorrow is another day and perhaps it will bring rain.

This morning I looked at the vegetable garden and decided we would either have to water it or abandon it for the summer. Watering is a day-long task and a terrific drain on even the best-flowing well. Yet we have never been able to pump enough from our deep well to check the flow, so I rigged the canvas "soaker" on the hose and kept it running for eight hours along the rows. Within hours, it seemed, the whole garden took a new lease on life, and perhaps this soaking will be enough to hold us until rain.

Last week we mowed one of the bottom fields that ordinarily is kept for pasture. It was a rough job and hard on the machinery, for here the creek breaks from its banks two or three times a year and brings in gravel; also the cattle had grazed here in the spring and left deep hoofmarks in the ground. The hay was not of the quality we like; yet Ern Stricklin brought his baler and the Williams boys came with their truck, and by noon on Saturday we had another four hundred bales in the barn.

It is hard to realize, when we get up in the cool of early morning, that we're facing another day in one of the hottest Junes we've known. Generally the thermometer stands in the low sixties and the sun, at this hour, casts long, cool shadows across the yard. But by the time breakfast is over, the morning breeze has turned to dry wind and the heat strikes down like a sword. Old Betsy waits at the stable door for Matt to come with the milk pail; and while he tends to his chores and feeds the calf, I spend a half hour in the garden with a hoe. Then we check the tractors for gas, oil, and water, fill up the drinking jug, and are off to the fields for the day's work. This week Matt is mowing the oats for hay while I plow out our corn patch. After it is cultivated, if the drought still holds, we'll roll it with the cultipacker to break up all clods and create a dust mulch on the surface of the ground. But rain will have to come within a day or two, for the leaves are "a'twistin' and a'hurtin'," as I once heard an Ozark youngster put it.

Sometimes I expect we complain when the weather is too wet. But in our hill country it is drought that brings real disaster to the farmer. Summer pasture and winter feed are our mainstays and neither will grow without rain.

july

Drought

Sometimes I believe that of all the vicissitudes a farmer can suffer—and goodness knows there are plenty of them—drought is the worst. During our years at Possum Trot Farm we have experienced most of the forms of natural disaster that can strike those who work on the land. Any one of them may leave devastation behind it, yet all except drought strike swiftly and are over.

We have had flash floods sweep through the bottomland fields to destroy the young corn. Lightning can kill the prize herd bull in an instant; a new plague of unsuspected insects may completely wipe out the first cutting of alfalfa; a freak windstorm lasting only seconds can lift the roof from the barn and deposit it in the next county. One or another of these things seems to be happening constantly to us or to some close neighbor—and they are things over which we have little or no control. Yet they happen and are finished; we can sit down after the event, assess the damage, make emergency plans, and start over.

When the flood subsides and the ground dries, we plant the corn again or substitute for it an emergency crop such as one of the grain sorghums. The neighbors band together and come in to help us reroof the barn. There is a second cutting of alfalfa on the way, which we protect by spraying. The chances are, we can line up enough credit to buy another herd bull.

Drought, however, is a different kind of disaster. It works by attrition—by a kind of wearing-away process that leaves the farmer's pocketbook, and very often his temper, thinner and thinner. There is something insidious about drought. In a farming country such as ours, where normal rainfall is forty-eight inches per year, a shortage of ten inches is serious, since our crops are based on the "normal." A sixteen-inch shortage means widespread crop failure, while a deficiency of twenty-four inches spells real disaster. Thus "drought disaster" seldom means *total* drought. Except in the most arid sections, there is always some precipitation; in a countryside such as ours this may mean single months with normal or even above-normal rainfall. These rains are like "fool's gold" in that they raise false hopes and persuade us to try again. We are now, at the end of five dry years, short something like one hundred inches in precipitation.

It was in 1952 that we first began to notice this rainfall shortage. At oat-planting time in March the ground was dry, which is a bad sign. Yet we did not think of it as especially serious until October, when farmers throughout the Ozark country found themselves without fall pasture. We had to bring in the cattle and start feeding them instead of letting them run out on the grass until almost Christmas. Yet a farmer cannot count on drought lasting forever. Ours is a business where there is no alternative to accepting the country axiom, "Of course it's going to rain again. It always has." Thus in the autumn of 1952 we went ahead with plans for putting in a field of new alfalfa and for seeding new pasture mixtures. This was not easy, for the cost of such seedings comes to nearly forty dollars per acre for tillage, seed, and fertilizer; and during that year the market price on our cattle dropped a full 40 per cent. Moreover, the price has stayed there ever since, with minor fluctuations.

When spring of 1953 arrived, it was plain the new seedings had not survived, so we planted again. This time, in addition, we hedged with emergency crops of oats and Sudan grass to help take the edge off the hay and pasture shortage. With cattle as the end product from our farm and prices greatly depressed, we could hardly afford to cut the number of animals we carry, although how to feed them became a constantly more difficult problem. But again the rains were short and again in autumn we planted—and again the winter went by with moisture far below normal.

It was during this next year, 1954, that we noticed the steady drop in subsoil moisture. Except for a few hours after the occasional rain it was no longer possible to dig fence-post holes in the rock-hard earth. Shallow ponds went dry that summer and the flow from springs and even from some deep wells was diminished. That was the summer, too, when we began to notice serious deterioration in our permanent pastures. The clover died out, as well as some of the hardy grasses, and their places were taken by annual and perennial weeds that live without regular rainfall. Once more we said to ourselves, "This is the season it has to break; this is the year it will start raining again." But of course it didn't. It got worse, instead.

During the fourth year even the deep ponds began to go dry and never-failing springs stopped flowing. In a hill country like ours, gravedigging is a task carried out by volunteers from among the neighbors of the deceased. When some of the old people died during that hot fourth summer, the gravediggers told us they found dry earth to the bottom of the graves. That was the summer the creeks stopped flowing aboveground and became a series of stagnant pools. Yields of all crops fell, some failed entirely, and, despite the use of emergency pasture and silage made from the dried-out corn, feed supplies were low when winter came. Some of the smaller farmers were closed out that year—not always because they were not good farmers, but because they did not have the reserves to hang on. Some larger farmers, though there was as much work to be done at home as ever, found part-time jobs. Others left for full-time work in the city while their wives and youngsters carried on at home as best they could.

Still the drought did not break. It rolled into its fifth year; and now, even when we could scrape together the wherewithal for seed, much of the ground was so hard it could not be worked. Yet perhaps this was just as well. In fields that had been in row crops last year and were thus loose enough to plow, the seed was planted again. And there it lay dormant, sometimes for weeks, until the first shower fell and it sprouted and died. By midsummer, water was becoming a real problem. Not only individual pastures but whole farms were out of water; and not only for livestock, but sometimes even for household use. Many farmers were forced to ship their livestock at bankruptcy prices. It will be necessary to start feeding those that are left long before the normal feeding season begins. Now most farmers are wondering whether their hay, grain, and silage can possibly hold out until another spring.

The whole effect of these conditions is enormously depressing. Here it is mid-July, in what should be the height of the growing season, and one hot, sunny day follows another without a break. Grass crackles underfoot like matchsticks when you walk through the fields. Streams are lower than they have ever been since the white man came to this country in the late 1700's —and each day they drop still more. Foresters tell us that by autumn, 365,000 acres of Ozark timber will be dead. Breeding cattle that should stay on the farms are shipped at losses that may never be retrieved—and experts who believe that shortages are the cure for low farm prices call these conditions "healthy."

All day long and every day the hot wind blows until we are tired of the sound and feel of it.

Somehow, despite these conditions, we hear little real complaint and little talk of giving up. Here are countless thousands of farmers with their backs to the wall because of conditions they could neither foresee nor prevent—and yet almost every one of them expects to stick it out, one way or another. This farming is a manufacturing business in which the owner and sole stockholder is also the manager and the labor force, yet a business in which he cannot set the prices at which he sells his products. It is a business in which a man builds up a considerable capital investment, yet feels himself fortunate to earn from it a minimum return on his labor. It is a business filled with all the risks the elements can bring to bear against it. Yet because of some strange perversity of human nature, it is a business we would not think of changing for any other.

Hound Music

Anyone who enjoys the music of the chase would enjoy this evening at Possum Trot, for tonight the fox hunters are abroad. Ken Moyer and Mon Hull and the Weeks boy and maybe some more have built their fire up at the foot of the mountain and unleashed their hounds. They must have struck almost at once and gone away to the north, around White's hill. Then the fox brought the pack south along our bluff until they were no more than a hundred yards from the house and the baying set Tiger and Mike into a frenzy of barking. But our dogs seem to know this is not their sport and soon quiet down to listen. The hounds "made a lose," as the foxhunter's phrase has it, and pottered around for perhaps ten minutes while some old veteran got the trail straightened out. Then away they went, hell-bent down the creek again, until the baying came drifting back to us as a muffled roar echoing from the granite walls of the Saline Creek "shut-ins." And I would rather be sitting out beside the foxhunter's fire on this fine July night than cooped up here at the typewriter.

Ginnie and I drove over to Belgrade, after supper, to get a set of fitted horseshoes for Daisy and Ribbon from our friend

Walter Gillam, who is just about the last of the good black-smiths in our country. We reached there just before dark and I left Ginnie visiting with Walter's wife while I went out and found him mowing the grass in the little Baptist Cemetery, just behind the house. The Gillams' boy, who was lost in the war, is buried there, and Walter and a neighbor spend an evening each week keeping the place neat. After they had finished, we sat for a while with the Gillams, talking about the old days when the lead mines were still operating out at Palmer settlement, west of Potosi, and many wagonloads of ore, railroad ties, and barrel staves were hauled out each day. Often there would be a dozen teams a day to be shod, and many a night Walter would be at the shop until ten o'clock, fitting shoes ready for the morning's work.

Our friend Bill Colman's dad was superintendent for the mining company, in those days, and there were many families living along Lost and Hazel and the other little creeks that make the Courtois and Huzzah rivers. And Walter told us about Tolliver Wingo, who headed the little Negro community in Strawberry Hollow, and whose son Watt is the only remaining survivor. Then we heard of the time when smallpox struck Potosi and the yellow quarantine flag was hoisted over part of the town to warn strangers away. My grandfather, "Doc Lem," took care of the patients, but they finally brought a doctor in from St. Louis to administer the new-fangled smallpox vaccine that has made this deadly disease almost a thing of the past. Now the Palmer settlement lies in the heart of the Clark National Forest, most of the people are gone, and the timber that was so ruthlessly stripped from those hills is beginning to grow again. A few trees are still cut on moonlight nights and each year some bad incendiary fires are strung along the ridges. But things grow gradually better and one day the forest will again yield a rich harvest to people who have learned how to conserve and use it wisely.

Often as I contemplate the handful of years in which we Americans have despoiled our resources, I am reminded of a statement made by naturalist Aldo Leopold, whose *A Sand County Almanac* is required reading for everyone with a serious interest in conservation. There is ample evidence, said Aldo, that wilderness (before "modern" man) maintained itself in balance for immensely long periods; that its component species were rarely lost, neither did they get out of hand; that weather and water built soil as fast or faster than it was carried away. Wilderness, then, assumes unexpected importance as a laboratory for the study of land health. When Leopold speaks of "tremendously long periods," he is talking in terms of tens of thousands of years.

Down in western New Mexico a group of archaeologists has spent eight summers studying the cultural history of the Cochise-Mogollon Indians, who formed one of three important early civilizations of the American southwest. This culture is not important for the height to which it rose, for it existed in an environment that was extremely rugged and poor in material resources. It is important, however, because it had an uninterrupted history that extended for more than twelve thousand years. What might be called the "higher culture" of the Cochise Indians began in 2500 B.C. and ended about 1300 A.D. But for all this tremendously long period, this primitive people existed and advanced slowly, meeting successfully each environmental change that came along. And these included a change in climate from the Pluvial Period, following the retreat of the glaciers of the Ice Age, to the semiarid condition that exists in that country today.

The Cochise-Mogollon culture did not rise as high as many that are known to history. Yet these people had a well-developed agriculture. They built towns or family communities that remained in existence for perhaps four thousand years. They were among the early developers of such crops as corn, beans, squash, and pumpkins. They were skilled hunters who knew the use of bow and spear and snare, and they discovered most of the knots that our Boy Scouts tie to earn their merit badges. They wove cloth, mats, and baskets and made beautifully decorated pottery. But most important of all, they lived on peaceful and cooperative terms with Nature. Thus they survived as a cultural entity for more hundreds of centuries than we can even reckon on the calendar of the vaunted white race.

Bursts of Blooms

Nature has a calendar of her own for the growing season on which the dates are marked off accurately by the blossoming of wildflowers. This calendar celebrates its New Year in early March when tiny bluets and Johnny-jump-ups appear in the fields, soon followed by hepatica, rue anemone, spring beauty, and a few more in the woodland. From then until mid-September in our Ozark country, never a week goes by which is not celebrated by the first opening of a dozen new flowers. April and May each bring a burst of bloom, but the busiest time of all is June, when a single day may be marked by as many as ten new blossoms.

This culmination of the flowering season in June is hardly to be wondered at, since most wildflowers operate on a time-table determined by day length. Flower buds of each species must be exposed to the light for an exact number of hours, absorbing the energy-giving rays of the sun, in order to unfold their petals. Thus it is natural that June twenty-first—the time of the summer solstice, when the hours of daylight are at their peak—probably sees more kinds of wildflowers in bloom than any other single day of the year. The list is far too long to set down here, but I think in our latitude it must total close to one hundred species, and even this figure may be conservative.

Living in the country the year round, you watch for these dates on the wildflower calendar just as you watch for the songbirds in spring and the wild geese in autumn. And July sees the blossoming of most of the plants that we think of as autumn flowers. A few of these are rare and delicate and very beautiful: nearly a dozen of our Missouri orchids, the Turk's-cap lily, *Lobelia cardinalis,* and the little rose pink with the botanical name of *Sabatia angularis.* But these do not grow along every roadside or in every field; they must be searched for with some knowledge of the hidden places where they bloom.

The majority of late summer flowers, especially the big showy ones, are more familiar to the casual traveler along the country roads. They are the wild sunflowers, cone flowers, Spanish needles, goldenrod of a half-dozen varieties, ironweed, the family of Eupatoriums, which include thoroughwort, boneset, Joe Pye weed, and white snakeroot. Then there are beggar's ticks, thistles, early asters, pennyroyal, and nearly a dozen of the mints. July is also the flowering season for the "sticktights," a dozen or so of our wild legumes that are classified as tick trefoils, and for senna and partridge pea. Actually, there are many more—the morning glories, sedges, guara, evening primrose, St. Johnswort, night-blooming catchfly, several milkweeds, and whole families of water plants.

Many of these flowers of midsummer are plants that have survived from an earlier day despite man's effort to eliminate from the landscape everything that cannot be turned into cash. This is why the majority of them are found growing in odd corners of the farm that are not reached by the mowing machine, or along country roads where the county highway funds are not quite large enough to cover eliminating them. Among these are the wild sunflowers, of which there are two dozen, and the compass plant, *Silphium laciniatum,* which grows as high as a man or higher and is topped with big yellow blooms much resembling the sunflowers. When buffalo roamed the bluestem prairies of the Ozarks on their eastward journeying, they must have traveled through a sea of yellow blossoms of the compass plant

—a wonderful sight, though there are few left to care that it will not be seen again. There is no profit in *Silphium*, we say, so let's spray it with herbicide and get rid of it. A weed—nothing more.

The naturalist who knows a bit of ecology might question this conclusion. He might point out that there are logical reasons for allowing the compass plant to occupy its odds and ends of wild land, and these in addition to its cheerful yellow flowers and the odd fact that the deeply cut leaves alternating on the tall stalk tend to point north and south, to which its name refers. *Silphium* is a real builder of soil fertility, with a huge sweet-potatolike root that goes down a dozen feet or more and has the typical characteristic of prairie plants that it can withstand the longest drought. It is also a long-lived perennial, taking perhaps ten years to reach flowering size and surviving to watch succeeding generations of farmers go to their reward. Year after year it pumps up minerals from the subsoil for the current year's growth; and as each autumn comes, these essential elements in the body of the plant are deposited in the topsoil.

Some agronomists have a tendency to belittle the value of such plants in the soil-building process; yet it is by mining the richness thus created through countless centuries that we have built our much-vaunted system of agriculture. One need only watch how cattle crop the wild plants in the pasture corners, obviously preferring them to the tame plants nearby, to realize that they are rich in the stuff that builds bone and muscle. And one need only study the steady decline in nutritive value of many of our farm crops, despite the yields in bushels or tons, to realize that even "scientific man" can still learn from Nature.

This is what we know: that a landscape untouched by man is a stable, life-producing organism, with the native plants and animals maintaining the steady flow of energy necessary to support this life; and that man's violent attack on this landscape often disrupts the natural equilibrium with effect more harmful than is intended or can be foreseen. The real problems that lie ahead for those who deal with land today are not problems involving bigger machines and heavier dosages of fertilizers, plant killers, and insecticides. They involve, rather a deeper understanding of ecology, that science which investigates the interrelationships between living organisms and their environments.

Old Swimming Hole

There have been few afternoons during the hot weather when young Ricky and I, sometimes with Ginnie along, have not managed to slip down to Saline Creek for a swim. Our swimming hole is pint-sized, just right for a boy of eight and yet deep enough so that his grandfather can float on his back to gaze up through green foliage to white clouds and a red-shouldered hawk sailing across the blue sky. The pool is located at the back of the farm, running down to the north watergap, and is set in a broad spot in the valley so that the current slows to a walk. Big trees grow along the banks: the finest burr and white oaks on the farm, giant sycamores, walnuts, and big honey locusts with feathery foliage.

We make no apology for these expeditions to the creek. Our farm day starts at six in the morning or sometimes earlier. When we are working in the bottom fields, especially, it takes no more than a minute at four o'clock to get to the stream. We laze for a half hour in water that is clear and cool enough to ease the day's fatigue and by five o'clock are back at the house, refreshed and ready for the evening chores and a couple of hours at the typewriter after supper.

I think people quite often wonder how we get our work done at Possum Trot, considering the time we spend picknicking. We go picknicking by utilizing the hours that other people spend at the dinner table and then watching television or going to the movies or the Little Symphony or the ball game. Our favorite places for outings are right here on the farm, so that we can leave the house at six o'clock and arrive at the picnic spot within ten minutes. There the woodpile is ready with a couple of big stones to serve for a fireplace, and the rest is as easy as eating at home.

One of the chief reasons we like to get out, aside from the relaxation, is that it gives us our best opportunity for sitting quietly to observe what is happening among the birds and other wild creatures on the farm. It is an odd thing, but the farmer who is by instinct something of a naturalist is the exception rather than the rule. When he does have leanings in this direction, he has both advantages and disadvantages in comparison with the city dweller. On the credit side, many of his waking hours are spent outdoors where interesting things are always happening in the woods and fields. On the debit side, however, these hours outdoors are generally filled to overflowing with tasks to be done. He must finish mowing the clover field, for example, just while the mother bobwhite hatches out her brood, and thus a wonderful opportunity for detailed observation is lost.

The professional naturalist, or even the amateur, concentrates his time in the field on observation. Many of our friends among the wildlife photographers will spend days in a blind at a single spot in order to get one photograph or a short motion-picture sequence. And despite the handicaps, there is an occasional farmer who becomes an expert in the field of natural history. Aldo Leopold tells, for example, of the Criddle brothers, wheat farmers on the broad Manitoba prairie. These two men became so interested in the wild fauna and flora of their ranch in a pioneering country that they eventually were recognized as outstanding authorities on everything from the botany to the wildlife cycles of their part of Canada. In the same way, a rancher in the mountains of New Mexico studied the elusive mountain lion and learned so much about it that he has written two of the most authoritative books on this animal.

Our own conclusion is that observing things in nature closely enough to know, understand, and enjoy them is largely a matter of using one's leisure time to this end. In the country we can do this, even when we cannot see the latest play or athletic contest. When one lives in the city, the problem is more difficult. Watching young fox kits playing at the mouth of their den or a hen mallard leading her brood through the marshy shallows, I am struck by the fact that there is more actual sport in studying wildlife and improving the carrying capacity of our land for quail, rabbits, racoon, and the rest than there is in killing them.

Fishing at Sunrise

Harvest pushes forward at such a pace that all our good resolutions not to neglect our fishing, horseback riding, and other extracurricular activities are in danger of going by the board. But this morning—it being the weekend and a day of rest—I awoke early. The sun was just topping the "low gap" in the mountain to the east. Quail were whistling all up and down the valley, a cheery call which is one of the dominant bird notes of summer. The clock struck five as I lay debating whether to turn over for another snooze or to head for the creek with the fly rod to see whether the sunfish were striking. The fly rod won and I dressed and headed down the road to the creek. A certain amount of stealth is necessary when starting out on such an expedition so as not to arouse the dogs. They love to go fishing—as they enjoy all our expeditions—but so far I have not been able to train them not to jump headlong into every likely hole before a single cast has been made.

Halfway down the hill I disturbed a pair of young cottontails playing tag in the road. Along the edge of the soybean field, a fat groundhog looked up from his breakfast and ambled without alarm toward his burrow at the edge of the bluff. And rounding the bend, I came upon a pair of bobwhites taking a dust bath in the road and watched them whir to the cover of the blackberry thicket. At the creek, the little green heron greeted me, walking up a slanting dead willow for a better view and then taking off downstream. We have been a long time without rain and the stream is low—so low that I can cross at the riffles without wetting my feet. To have any luck on such a morning, when the water is crystal clear and the shadows are long and the holes have shrunk to the size of a pocket handkerchief, one must stalk the quarry with skill and care. But this makes the game more fun.

My custom on these small excursions is to start fishing a short distance above our ford where there are several likely holes, even though these are worked over almost daily by bank fishermen of all sizes and descriptions. From this point I work downstream until there are enough fish in the creel for our modest requirements—or until I am convinced that the fish are not striking.

Up opposite Matt's gate, at the very edge of the road, a gnarled old willow leans above the stream at the lower end of a gravel run. Here the driftwood carried down by high waters has lodged and a pool of respectable size and depth has formed. It is a likely spot and, although it has not proved productive in the past, reports have come in of a good-sized smallmouth bass that makes his abode here and spurns all offerings of worms and minnows. I generally like to fish such spots from above; but this would mean wading to the other side with the resulting disturbance of the water, plus the difficulty of keeping my shadow from falling across the pool. So I stood at the tail of the pool in the deep shadow, stripped out a good length of line, and dropped the fly with a long cast well above the willow roots. Carefully I let the lure settle, then worked it along just fast enough to keep the spinner turning. Nothing happened until I was almost ready to lift the fly to the surface for another cast. Then, at the very tail of the pool, came the unmistakable strike of a "sunnie." I hustled him out onto the gravel bank and popped him into the creel, since he was of good eating size.

Generally, when the stream is so low, a single rise from a pool is about all one can expect; the disturbance kicked up by the hooked fish is enough to send his brethren scurrying to cover. That could hardly have happened in this case, however, since my sunfish rose at the very end of the retrieve. So I waited for a moment and dropped the fly again, a bit farther upstream than before. Nothing happened on the first or second cast. But on the third, as I worked the lure carefully past the drift, there came a solid, smashing strike. The situation was ticklish for a moment, for the bass started headlong toward the roots. Once he got there, my light leader wouldn't last a minute. But the fish made a fatal mistake. He charged to the surface to shake out the hook. A flip of the rod tip and I had him turned out into the pool and downstream, away from the roots and snags. I worked him toward the shallows and shortly he also was resting safely in the creel.

I won't break any records with this fish. But he is my best out of our small creek this year. His fourteen inches filled the creel from end to end. Some fifty yards downstream, I missed another that would have been his match. He was chasing minnows out through the shallows, then cruising back to a retreat so overhung with branches that to drop a fly into it was all but impossible. So I contented myself with four more sunnies and was back at home before seven, in time to clean my catch for Ginnie's skillet and an early breakfast.

august

The Pond

The late Robert Coffin, who wrote of the salt-water farms of Maine, has a poem I've always liked. He tells of the farmer who rocked his troubles away in a favorite rocking chair. This chair crept across the floor as he rocked, from wall to fireplace, and by the time the old fellow had made the journey twice he was at peace with the world; ready for bed and whatever fortune tomorrow might bring.

Here at Possum Trot Farm we have a somewhat similar technique for ironing out our troubles, though in a little different way. When the bottom drops out of the cattle market while tractor prices go higher or aphids take the alfalfa or bugs strip the vegetable garden in spite of dusting, we find that our remedy is almost sure fire. I tell Ginnie to pack her picnic basket and the old camp coffee pot. Then we hurry through the evening chores, load the red setters into the car along with the creel and fly rod, and head down the county road and across the fields to the Big Pond.

This Big Pond of ours could hardly be called an impressive body of water. It covers, in fact, just about an acre and a half. Yet it is one of the most peaceful places I know, especially in early morning or in the evening along about sunset. It is far

from the house and the highway—set at the edge of a broad
and sloping meadow where fat Herefords graze contentedly.
And we feel about these Herefords as does our friend the sheriff
of a neighboring county who came to visit one day.

"I'll tell you, Len," he said, as we looked over the herd
and he approved the good points of each animal. "Those cattle
are mighty fine property for a feller to own—even if they
weren't worth a dime."

So, no matter what their market price, white-faced cows
and calves on a green pasture make a picture we always enjoy
contemplating.

Over to the west of the Big Pond, at a distance of perhaps
three hundred yards, Saline Creek flows down its wooded course,
flanked on the far side by a high limestone bluff behind which
the sun sets early. But a mile to the east, where Buford Mountain raises its rounded crest, the glow lingers for moments
longer while purple shadows creep up the deep hollows on its
slopes. It is the hour when tree and bank swallows come to
harvest insects above the water, dipping now and then to break
the surface. And high above them, still in bright sunlight, the
nighthawks wheel and dive in graceful, erratic flight.

Once at the pond, we build a small Indian fire between
two stones and set the coffee to boil. Then, while Ginnie brings
out the provender of her basket, I tie on a floating lure to make
a few casts for one of the big bass that live under the old snag
where the water is deep. Four or five pounds these fellows run,
so that one of them is excitement enough for an evening. Then
I come back to the campfire and watch the fireflies turn on their
small lanterns. A barred owl calls from the woods—Old Eight-
Hooter is his country name. Stars begin to wink out overhead
and the day's cares are forgotten

A farm pond is something you build. Its purpose, generally,
is to create a supply of water for livestock in some field where

you need it—or for the farm buildings, except the drinking water—or even as a reservoir for irrigation. This latter, however, takes a deep pond with a big storage capacity. Compared with our small livestock ponds, the irrigation reservoir is expensive. We have seven ponds at Possum Trot, most of them small and serving only to water livestock, and all of them built since we came here ten years ago. The Big Pond, however, has other uses, which will be explained presently.

It really isn't difficult to plan and build a farm pond. You decide, first of all, where you want or need a supply of water. Then it is well to have someone with experience make a few borings with a soil augur or posthole digger to be sure the soil structure is such that it will become watertight after saturation. You would not want to dig a pond, for example, where you might hit rock close to the surface or where there is a loose gravelly subsoil that simply won't hold water. The most successful farm ponds depend entirely on surface runoff from rainfall for their water supply, so that the next step is to be certain you have a watershed of sufficient size draining into the pond. It must be large enough, in other words, so that the normal rainfall of your region will keep the pond filled; yet should not drain so large an area that there is recurring danger of washing away the earthen fill that you make to serve as a dam. You'll have a better water supply, too, if rainfall drains in over a good grass sod, rather than over cultivated ground, since the sod acts as a filter to keep the water clear.

There are many reasons why surface drainage from rainfall, rather than the flow from a stream or spring, makes for an ideal farm pond. Streams have a way of flooding in times of heavy rainfall and this constitutes a danger to the dam, this same thing applying, in lesser degree, to the flow from a spring. Sometimes if a pond is built over a spring, the very weight of water above will cause its flow to stop, so that it breaks out at some other point, generally below the pond dam.

But the chief drawback is that a constant supply of fresh water flowing into and through the pond has a tendency to keep it sterile, that is, low in the organic matter and in all of the minute organisms that are its very life. The pond depending on rainfall for its water supply will support more aquatic life and has a greater producing capacity than one supplied by a running stream or spring.

There are plenty of people who can help with the details of pond planning and building: the county Extension Agent, the U.S. Soil Conservation Service engineer, a field man from the Fish and Wildlife Commission, or an experienced dirt-moving contractor who has built other ponds. Any of these can help with final selection of the location, with necessary surveying of the watershed, and with staking out the earth fill and spillway. With some knowledge of the size of dam, depth of water wanted, and rates per hour for dirt-moving equipment, they can also give a close estimate of costs.

The chief rules to remember, other than those already

given, are to have the pond deep enough (approximately ten feet in the deep water area), and to provide a sodded spillway big enough to handle overflow during periods of heavy rainfall. Also if you intend using the pond for livestock water, plan for a pipe through the dam with a watering tank outside. You can fence the pond against trampling by animals and thus prevent erosion, silting, and contamination.

When we built our Big Pond, we knew that we wanted to stock it with fish and also to create around it the best possible conditions for all forms of wildlife likely to use such an area. First step was to manure the dam heavily and seed it to pasture grasses and the big perennial legume called sericea lespedeza, which grows six feet tall and provides dense cover, as well as some food, for songbirds, bobwhite, and the small furbearers. Then we built a fence around the pond, taking in an area of perhaps three acres, and here nothing was done except to spread some commercial fertilizer.

Once the pond had filled, the next step was to stock it with fish, and this was done by our state Conservation Commission, who brought in and released about a thousand bluegill fry and two hundred fingerlings of the largemouth bass. This was done without cost, in return for our agreement to allow a reasonable amount of controlled fishing by our neighbors. Heavy fishing pressure on the farm pond—once the fish population has established itself—is altogether essential; without it, both bass and bluegill will multiply to the point of overpopulation and eventual starvation. The Commission also recommended an annual application of fertilizer to encourage microscopic plant growth, thus providing food and cover for the small organisms that are at the base of the pond "food chain": plankton, small crustaceans, insect larvae, nymphs, bluegills, bass.

The fish in a well-managed pond increase in size at an astonishing rate; and meanwhile, in the small area of wild land surrounding it, all sorts of interesting things begin to happen.

A blackberry thicket spreads and grows; seedlings of multi-flora rose appear along the fences where birds drop the seed; grass thrives tall and rank. A few willows take hold at the outside base of the dam and other trees show up in the enclosure: ash, winged elm, hickory, and cedar.A clump of sumac sprouts near the blackberry.

When spring arrives, the migrating waterfowl start dropping in. There are bands of blue and snow geese that rest on the pond and go out to graze in the fields of wheat and barley. Visiting ducks include the little teal, scaup, gadwall, ringneck, baldpate, shoveler, wood duck, and mallard. Shorebirds feed along the marshy edges of the pond: greater and lesser yellowlegs, Wilson's snipe, woodcock, sandpipers. The herons come to fish the pond and stay all summer, the great blue and little green and the American and least bitterns. The rattle of the kingfisher is a familiar summer sound. Bobwhites raise their young in the blackberry thicket and red-winged blackbirds nest in the button bushes. Kingbirds and flycatchers and phoebes frequent the pond area, as do the nighthawks and swallows.

All of the animal kingdom seems attracted to this small bit of wild land and water—and this with little planning or effort on our part. A pair of muskrats move in from the creek; we view these with some misgiving, since they burrow into the pond dam. Big snapping turtles take up residence, as well as harmless water snakes. Frogs come in countless numbers to lay their eggs in the shallows, little hyla crucifer, the "spring peeper," the lyrical garden toad, green and meadow and leopard frogs, and finally the big bullfrogs whose voices we can hear plainly, a half-mile away across the fields, long after we've come home to bed. Always along the water's edge we find tracks of the raccoon, an enthusiastic fisherman; and more than once, as we've sat beside our small fire, the eerie, sardonic laugh of the red fox has come floating to us across the water.

The farm pond, it seems to me, is one of the best examples

of what can happen when man works hand in hand with nature
—in this enterprise, at least up to a point, by rather intensive
human management. We select the place to put the pond where
it will do the most good for our own selfish purposes. Then
we go in and completely upset the landscape for a time with
our bulldozers and scoops; but at once start again to re-create
the natural conditions. What we are doing, actually, is to build
here a small new "biotic community" in which many niches are
unfilled. The pond is fertilized and stocked with fish; this much
is artificial, for the fish population must be kept in balance.
But the rest of the things just happen. Here are good conditions
of food and shelter for insects, certain reptiles, amphibians,
birds, and animals; and it is not long before they take advantage
of these. Here is a safe resting ground for the migrants, tired
from journeying the long skyways, and down they come to visit
us.

The fishing alone can make our Big Pond one of the most
productive areas, acre for acre, on this whole farm. But there
are many other values that accrue almost automatically. Besides
the animals who come to stay, neighborhood youngsters come
with their cane poles (and often with their parents) to catch
bluegills by the dozens. To our family, the Big Pond is a sure
refuge against those pressures of modern life which reach out
to the farm just as surely as they do into the city apartment. It
is our best proof, too, that we are still part of the community
of Nature—and that she responds richly to our efforts to live
in harmony with her.

Country Sounds

Often we talk about the quiet of the country, and indeed,
when we compare it with the snarling roar during the hours of
peak traffic in the city, the country does seem a quiet place. Yet
when we catalogue the familiar sounds of a summer day on the

farm, it is obvious that the rural scene knows little absolute silence. Most of the sounds are both soothing and beautiful. Many of them, moreover, recall far-off days and the pleasant scenes of childhood—the orchard, the meadow, the deep-tangled wildwood.

Sometimes I wake early, before there is any hint of dawn, and look out the window to see the planet Venus hanging in the eastern sky. When she appears at her brightest, she far out-shines Sirius, the brightest star—you will be rewarded by look-ing at her through a small telescope or pair of powerful field glasses. For now Venus will appear in crescent form, like a miniature moon, and many times larger than when we see her as a full planet. At this hour the night insects have largely ceased their singing and the silence of the countryside is per-haps as complete as it ever becomes. But soon, from one farm after another in the neighborhood, we hear the roosters crow-ing, a symbol of morning that is as old as the history of man-kind.

Down in the pasture a calf that has been tucked safely into a fencerow to sleep, while its mother takes advantage of the coolness to graze, begins to bawl. The cow answers and the calf moves toward her, with breakfast in prospect. Then I hear another, and another, and then in the woods along the bluff there starts a sleepy murmuring of bird song. Perhaps it is the first soft whistle of the cardinal that disturbs the yellow breasted chat; and this lusty fellow comes completely awake without any gentle preliminaries, bursting into full-throated song that, if not exactly musical, is at least of infinite variety.

From deeper in the woods comes the plaintive, questioning sigh of the wood pewee, followed by the harsh call of a black-billed cuckoo. The cardinal, which started this whole chorus with his first whisper, now has the sleep out of his eyes. He stretches his wings, flies to the top of the tallest tree in the neighborhood, and greets the approaching sun with a ringing "Cheer, cheer, what cheer." Off in the east, now, the day comes swiftly. Clouds above the mountain are turning pink and strong rays of light streak upward into the sky. Down at the handle mill, the five-o'clock whistle blows; as the echo dies, if we listen closely we may hear the howl of a wolf, away over on the edge of the valley. A neighbor starts calling his milk cows in a musical voice, and it is morning.

All through the sunny day, there is a variety of sounds in the summer scene. You hear the tractors starting up, the steady "thump-thump" of a hay baler, and the high whine of a chain saw cutting timber. Hens sing in the poultry runs and cackle themselves hoarse at the triumph of each egg, as if no egg had ever been laid before. And all day long, like a Greek chorus, these other sounds come to us against the background of the cicadas. The big robust insects emerge from the earth where they have spent from four to seventeen years as burrowing, root-feeding nymphs, finally crawling up some rough-barked tree to split their skins and come forth to dry their wings.

The somewhat sad whirring of the locust is certainly a dominant sound of our midwestern summers. It begins early in the morning, continues unabated throughout the day, and rises to a tremendous crescendo as dusk approaches. At this hour it drowns out all the other insects for a time and seems determined to dominate even the radio that is broadcasting the day's news.

Most of our songbirds are quiet during the midday hours in summer. Bobwhite whistles in morning and evening. Our wrens can be heard chattering throughout the day, especially if old Veronica, the cat, is dozing anywhere in the yard, but confine their singing to the hours of dawn and dusk. Field and song sparrows are heard at these hours, but the bright little indigo bunting sings throughout the day. Often, after darkness has fallen and the songs of cricket and katydid have supplanted those of the cicada, we are conscious of the twittering of the chimney swifts and the harsh cry of the nighthawk. And almost always, if we're sitting outdoors, we are treated to a concert by the mockingbird. Then a barred owl booms his call from the deep woods and away over toward the mountain we hear the hounds strike the trail of a red fox. The yellow-breasted chat gives one final sleepy performance and we know it is time for a farmer to start to bed.

Mowing Clover

Even when the weather is at its hottest, there is no job on the farm I enjoy more than mowing a field of clover. There is little need at this time of year to wait for the dew to dry, since the hot sun will easily take up the moisture from the hay in the mowed swath. So I check the mower on the evening before the haying starts, making certain the sickle is sharp and all the sections tight in the sickle bar. The tractor is greased and oiled and filled with gas. Then, if the day for mowing is clear, the chores are finished and I am on my way to the field by seven o'clock.

The particular clover field we mowed this week is down across the creek at the back of the farm, about three quarters of a mile from the house, and at this hour of day I even enjoy the trip that is necessary to get there. Along the county road, which dips sharply into the bottom, the undergrowth is dense now and makes wonderful cover for the birds and cottontails. A yellow-billed cuckoo slips silently across on graceful wings as I go and a pair of quail are dusting at the turn of the road. Brilliant little indigo buntings sing from the phone wires, and from the alfalfa field comes the sharp alarm whistle of a fat groundhog. At the creek the kingfisher perches in his usual place on the water-gap cable and a family of little green herons take off and disappear into the willows as I cross.

Once on the far side of the creek, I turn in at our gate and take a quick check of the cows and calves in the pasture there, making a mental note that, the first early morning we can line up a little extra help, we must move the big steers to new graz-

ing. At the back of the farm I follow the hedge fence of multi-flora rose that runs down to the clover field, and am soon inside. When you work on the land month after month and year after year, you are hardly conscious of the changes that take place, and this is true whether the condition of the land is going up or down. I recall Aldo Leopold pointing out that no tourist and few ranchers who live in the great Southwest are conscious of the deterioration of that countryside from good range to pic-turesque and colorful desert in a space of not much more than fifty years.

This field where I was mowing is, without undue boasting, a good example of land going upward in fertility and life-carrying capacity. When we first came to Possum Trot it was producing a fair crop of "poor Joe," the little lance-leaved rag-weed that has the ability to mine a living from infertile soil, and broom sedge, which is the last stand of wornout fields. These are true poverty plants, yet they have a certain virtue. Both are so unpalatable that livestock will hardly eat them and thus they give the land a rest. Moreover, through the simple process of growth and decay, they bring up mineral elements from the soil and deposit these as organic matter in the upper layers. Thus over a long period of years—perhaps fifty to a hundred or even longer—the land has a chance to recover so that better and more palatable plants move in again.

We tried a wheat crop with a seeding of grass and clover on this field during our first season at the farm, and both were a failure. Then we went to work with lime, fertilizer, and green manure until finally, just before the drought struck, we had got the land into fair production. Last autumn we tried again, with barley for a nurse crop and a seeding of red and alsike clover, sweet clover, alfalfa, lespedeza, and orchard grass, fescue, and timothy. We used the barley for spring pasture, then mowed the remnants so the grass and legumes could come along evenly. This week the field was ready for its second mowing—and for a farmer it would have been hard to find a more beautiful sight. The growth was lush and rank and the air heavy with the scent of many-colored blossoms.

I searched out a good shade for my water jug, lowered the sickle bar on the mower, laid off the field into two lands with my eye, and cut the back swath. Then the day's work really started. Our Ferguson mower is a revolutionary farm tool that drives its cutting blade from a counter-balanced crankshaft, instead of the old-fashioned wooden or iron Pitmann rod, and runs almost without vibration. Round and round I went while the sun climbed higher and the perspiration fogged my spectacles and dripped in a steady stream from my nose. But the first land grew narrower with each round and by midmorning was finished.

At its southern end, the clover field borders the Big Pond and on nearly every round a pair of beautiful American egrets, disturbed at their fishing, would rise to make a slow circle with the sunlight glistening on their snowy plumage. I keep an eye out for ripples in the grass ahead of the blade, which mark the scared flight of a young cottontail. It takes a moment to stop the machine and chase these little fellows out across the swaths of mowed hay to safety, but is well worth the effort. And there were no bobwhites nesting in the field, which is a good sign that the hatch was early. Along toward noon the swallows came to feed on insects rising from the cut swaths. These graceful flyers with their swift wingbeat seem to know that man means them no harm and so they swoop and dart within a foot or two of my head.

Along toward noon the second land was more than half finished and I saw Ginnie and Ricky driving across the pasture. We had planned a quick swim in Saline Creek and then luncheon on the gravel bar; and with only an hour's mowing left for the afternoon I was glad enough to pull into the shade, shut off the engine, and climb down to stretch. Ern Stricklin was coming to bale next afternoon, and I knew from the feel of the swaths which had been first mowed that the field would be ready to rake in the morning as soon as the dew dried. And I went down to the creek with the comfortable feeling any farmer has when he knows the barns are gradually being filled and that the cattle will be well fed this coming winter.

Feeders

This evening at sundown, I took the fly rod and went to the creek to try my luck. The stream is so low, now, that there are stretches where it runs for many yards beneath the gravel, and the fish have collected in the deeper holes that still give them some cover and where the water stays comparatively cool. When I walk along the bank and look down into these crystal-clear pools, standing still for long enough so that the fish are not startled, I am always amazed at the number of bass that manage to survive in a stream that is supposedly "fished out."

I have long been convinced, however, that poor fishing is far more a matter of poor conditions on our streams than it is of the number of fishermen.

On the other hand, the concentration of fish that occurs during a drought does not make for better fishing; all you need do is to alarm the smallest sunfish in the pool and your chances of taking any fish at all go glimmering. A few yards below where I was casting my fly, the pool runs out into a broad shallow that is no more than a few inches deep. Here the trailing branches of a leaning sycamore dip the water's surface. On one of these branches a cicada was singing and making a considerable fuss about it. Suddenly there was a boil in the water beneath him and a bass of good size leaped clear of the water in an obvious attempt to seize this morsel.

The bass jumped several times and missed. Then the cicada made a fatal mistake. He took off, perhaps four inches above the water, for a safer place from which to continue his concert. He had flown perhaps three feet and was starting to gain a bit of altitude when the bass made his final leap. The cicada disappeared, his song cut off in mid-flight, and the water showed a V as the bass headed for his home under the bank.

I had stood quite still as this small drama was carried out, and now was suddenly conscious of another slight disturbance along the gravel bar, just downstream. It was the unmistakable small talk and chatter of a covey of quail. I turned to see the whole family heading from the cover of the willows down to an inlet to drink. We have watched this covey ever since it hatched in the woods pasture close by and wondered how many would survive, so close to the road. Twice I had found where one of the birds had been captured and eaten—and my surmise as to the predator has been the Cooper's hawk, which makes this small woodland its hunting ground. The spot is ideal for the hawk because Matt's young White Rock chickens range down this way and several of them, nearly up to frying size, have recently disappeared. Now, as I stood there watching the quail drinking, a thunderbolt struck in the midst of the covey. The hawk had evidently been lurking in a nearby tree. As he struck, I must have flung up an arm; for he missed his aim, and the quail whirred off in every direction.

Right now I have a crick in my neck. Last night after supper, Ginnie and I sat on the west terrace to rest awhile and watch the sunset and the cattle grazing out along the ridge.

We were enjoying the sights and sounds and the coolness that steals along our valley at sunset when a small object fell past my chair, catching my attention out of the corner of an eye. Suddenly it came past again, but this time moving upward. It was a small brownish-gray spider of the family of orb weavers, which spins a new web each night.

We have watched it often before, yet if there is any more wonderful performance in nature than this one, I would be hard put to name it. This small spider was ambitious, for the web supports were swung a full six feet, down from the eaves to a porch chair, then back up to the wires where the power line enters the house. And the spot it has selected for its nightly spinning is just outside the kitchen window where the light will be certain to attract a plentiful supply of insects.

Darkness had fallen by the time the spider was ready for a real start, so we brought a flashlight and played it on the small creature as it worked. Such an industrious and business-like performance you never saw. Once the anchoring strands of web had been spun, it started work on the radial strands, crossing these in the center at a small anchorage that looked like a knot of silken thread. Later we determined that there were twenty-four of these radial strands, nor did the spider stop for even a moment when it had finished these.

Next step was to weave the net itself, and round and round it went, spinning with incredible rapidity. As the newly spun strands appeared, they glistened in our beam of light, then gradually became duller. Perhaps a dozen trips were made around the circumference of the web, with strands fastened a quarter inch apart.

Then additional strands were strung and fastened between these and the whole process repeated again and again until the center of the web was reached. We estimated the web to be sixty inches in circumference and that the spider had made sixty to eighty trips around it, each trip slightly shorter than the one before, until it reached the center; and that every strand must be fastened twenty-four times on each round to the radial supports.

The moment the web was finished, the spider became motionless in its center; nor was it long before small insects began to find their way into the net so skillfully spread for them.

AUTUMN

september

Nothing Really Dies

Sometimes at sunset on clear days we see the vapor trails of
the big jets tracing golden ribbons across the western sky. Yet
fast as they travel it often seems to us that time flies faster.
Just yesterday it was spring and we were arriving home from
the Caribbean to find the first hepaticas blooming in the woods.
Looking back at it, summer seems a kaleidoscope of haying and
horseback riding, herding cows and vaccinating calves, swimming and picnicking, which ended for us with a small boy in
a ten-gallon hat climbing the gangplank of a Stratoliner bound
for San Francisco. For all we could tell, he was as nonchalant
about it as we might have been, back in 1910 or thereabouts,
climbing aboard a one-horse surrey.

Most of Ricky's summer is made up of the sort of things
our grandfathers and grandmothers gave us. My grandfather
Doc Lem, who had served his time in the Confederate cavalry,
taught me to ride. "Seat low and shoulders high," he would say,
"and no slack in your reins." So we pass it on to Rick and he
sits old Ribbon like a veteran. His swimming hole in Saline
Creek is not many miles from the one where I learned to dog-
paddle, long years ago, and I'm sure the crop of chiggers he
picked up in the blackberry patch this summer are lineal

descendants of the ones I scratched as a boy.

Rick learned this vacation that a nighthawk has swept-back wings like a Navy fighter and that the turkey buzzard is black from underneath as it soars overhead, while the hawks are gray. He observed that a cat kills an occasional bird or lizard to eat, as part of the orderly process of nature, but that this is no reason why a youngster should kill either birds or lizards. Lightning bugs' lanterns are at their best, he agreed, when they twinkle high in the air, not when they are torn from the body of the owner and dropped into a bottle. And a three-inch sunfish caught and returned to the creek to grow is as exciting as one brought home to eat. Things like this are good for a boy to know, as well as the competitive sports we set so much store by. They are even more valuable, it seems to me, in building some determination to defend his small fortress of individuality against the forces of conformity that press in upon us.

Now summer is about gone. Last week we saw the first flight of blue-winged teal flashing above the pond. Horse-chestnut trees have lost their leaves and the rough-hulled buck-eyes hang from the bare limbs. When we walk out into the high meadows in the evening for a last look at the heifers, plovers rise whistling into the twilight to circle and land again. Identification in the dusk is difficult, but from the call notes and the silhouettes against the sky we can identify the black-bellied plover, the upland plover, and the long-billed curlew, which is becoming quite rare.

It has never seemed to me, though, that autumn is an ending; for when you live close to the land, you realize that nothing really dies. Perennial plants wither, yet the root lives and often even puts out a rosette of leaves before winter comes, to foretell next year's growth. In the seed of each annual plant is stored up life for the season ahead. Autumn is a time of harvest and gar-nering, of waterfowl flying south, of groundhogs storing fat for the winter sleep, and squirrels and chipmunks filling their warehouses against cold weather. It is a time of planting and planning for the farmer as he makes ready for next year's crops and lambs and calves. It is a time when we look forward to a cessation of hard work—altogether, one of the finest seasons of the year.

Storekeeper

Our old friend George Wallace, whom I've known since boyhood, has passed to his reward. With his passing, a certain spark has gone from the little town of Old Mines. In this ancient village, which was once a center of Missouri's leadmining industry and is now the heart of one of the world's great barite deposits, George kept store for just about forty years. And his was the very essence of all country stores. Moreover, its location always interested me. I don't mean by this the fact that it stood for so long beside Old Mines Creek at the junction of the highway and the gravel road leading to Cadet. George Wallace, like many people whose families settled early in this part of Missouri, came from Scotch Presbyterian stock. But Old Mines itself is French. Clustered around the town and up and down each creek valley thereabouts are several hundred families of pure French extraction. They are descendants of Brittany miners who came here with Renault and other French entrepreneurs to exploit the mineral resources of the region away back in the early 1700's.

Most of what has been written of these people has had to do with their hard economic lot since machinery came to replace hand mining in taking out the surface deposits of barite ore, which has always been known locally as "tiff." Remembering earlier days, I would say that tiff mining was never a lucrative profession for the miner, even in the time when it was dug with pick and shovel and hauled up out of the shaft in a wooden bucket on a hand-operated windlass. But there is another story to be told about the people of Old Mines, for they represent one of the most interesting group survivals left in America. It will be too bad when all the old people are gone and the automobile and the highways have wiped out the last of the semi-isolation that enabled them to keep alive old ways and customs for more than two hundred years.

The congregation of St. Joachim's Church is one of the oldest Catholic congregations in Missouri. The present church of soft red brick that stands close above the highway dates back to 1830, but it is not the first building on the site. It is spiritual headquarters for all the French families thereabouts. But just as the Church of St. Joachim is spiritual headquarters for the people of Old Mines, I think it could justly be said that George

Wallace's store was temporal headquarters. From the temporal point of view, I think George stood *in loco parentis* to the whole community. He was postmaster and unofficial mayor who never needed to be reelected. He was also unofficial banker and lawyer. He advised and arbitrated. When war came, it was George who must carry good news and bad. He guided his people through the coils of red tape surrounding allotments, insurance, and other governmental mysteries. If old Aunt Luce did not appear at the store on Wednesday, which was her day to take home a "poke" of groceries and a twist of Granger for Uncle Paul, it was George who sent out a grandnephew of the tribe to find out the trouble—or as often simply dispatched a basket of groceries. It was George who tided them over hard times, whether brought on by illness or slack work in the mines. And I think it would be unjust not to say that I understand he collected his debts in due time.

George's store on Saturday was a thing to see. In one corner the post office went full blast. Work shoes and overalls, sunbonnets and gingham by the yard, lard buckets and steel traps, ax hafts and pick handles, flour and salt pork, candy out of a wooden bucket, chewing tobacco in twists and plugs, roofing paper to cover the sides of a log cabin from which the chinking is falling, lengths of stovepipe and sorghum in season—such were the staples of Saturday trade. Here old men met to talk around the stove, and the old women to gossip about their grandchildren.

And always, booming throughout the store, came the voice of George. The smile on his long, lean face was as wide as a harvest moon and the stories he loved to tell were laughed at no less heartily because they had been told every Saturday for a quarter of a century. It was George's voice that stirred the laughter, for it was an all-embracing voice, friendly and itself full of laughter.

George had many side interests. If I recall rightly, he was an early owner of a country telephone line in the days when the proprietor went along with his "line gang" to string wire on the fence posts. He owned a "picture show" in the days when movies were newer than they are today. Always George was something of a farmer, and I suppose he operated a farm or two until the end. He was still a foxhunter in the Ozark sense, and could sit of an evening on the back gallery of his house and listen to a fox race. A likely Walker or Redbone pup would bring an appreciative gleam to his eye.

I can remember that in my earliest days George was a great bird hunter with a yard always full of good pointers. It had not been my good fortune to spend much time afield with him, but from our talks I know George was a close and accurate observer of all nature's phenomena. Most interesting to me is that, unlike too many sportsmen who know it all from spending a few days afield each year, George's conclusions from a long life spent close to Nature tallied with those of men trained in the field of scientific wildlife management. For this quality extremely rare in the layman I salute him.

Living off the Country

On a sunny September afternoon we were hiking along the banks of Saline Creek with friends from town and the subject came up of "living off the country." This would be difficult to do, we decided, especially for one person alone and in any place where the destructive hand of the white man has rested heavily for a century and a half. Yet if the attempt had to be made, I think autumn would be as good a time as any to make it. For autumn is the time of Nature's richest harvest, when a walk through the woods will reveal many sources of food even to the amateur naturalist. Still I would say that the task of taking one's livelihood from the wild land would be much easier if one had a bit of fishing tackle, a light rifle or shotgun, matches, condiments, cooking utensils, and (for really tasty dishes) a gallon or so of lard or bacon fat for seasoning.

There are, of course, some fruits of the forest that do not become edible until hard frost, while others are just now at their peak. On our walk we found, for example, that the wild grapes are turning ripe and hanging in dark clusters from ancient vines that climb to the tops of the highest trees, sometimes strangling them to death. The grapes are edible, though a trifle sour, still needing a frosty night or two to convert the juice to sugar. Yet now is when they should be gathered for making wild-grape jelly, which has a fine, tangy flavor that goes well with any sort of game. Later on, when frost has sweetened them, it is almost impossible to get them to jell.

Elderberries are another fruit that must be gathered before frost. This is a versatile wild plant, for a light wine can be made from the blossoms, which are also sometimes dipped in a batter and fried. The stems, which are hollow, were once used to make "spiles" for collecting maple syrup. Right now the bushes are loaded with great clusters of purple fruit from which country folk like to make at least a pie or two and a few glasses of jelly.

Most forms of wildlife share in the elderberry crop—quail, doves, songbirds, deer, wild turkey, and fox squirrel—while cattle browse freely on the leaves and twigs. And this is also the case with our persimmon, although this fruit of autumn needs—with the exception of an occasional and rarely discovered tree—a few really frosty nights to turn it sweet and take out the pucker.

Still another autumn fruit is the blackhaw, *Viburnum prunifolium*, which has a frosty dark-blue fruit with a pleasant taste. This can also be used for making jelly, though the juice of some tart fruit such as crabapple must be added to give it flavor. Again, it is used by many forms of wildlife and, besides being a decidedly ornamental small tree for use in the yard, will help attract the songbirds.

On our walk along the creek we discovered that the papaws are beginning to ripen, and it was plain to see, from those which had fallen to the ground, that they were being eaten by both birds and furbearers. The fruit of the papaw is at its best after a light frost or two, which turns it on the outside from green to yellow to a dark brownish-blue in color. It is palatable enough to appear in local markets where the plant is native. The fruits are fat and kidney-shaped, generally appearing in the tree in clusters of two to four; and while the taste is difficult to describe, it is a bit like papaya with a touch of ripe persimmon and banana added.

It takes a good frost or two to ripen walnuts, hickory nuts, and hazelnuts—all of which grow in our Ozark woodland and would play an important part in a "live off the land" diet. Acorns from the many varieties of oak are all too high in tannin to be palatable, except those of the chinquapin, though in years of food shortage all kinds were soaked and roasted and ground into meal by both Indians and settlers on the frontier. Spring rains helped the flowering of the nut-bearing trees and they have more fruit than during the worst drought years. Yet I would still call this season's crop a short one.

The ingenious woodsman could doubtless contrive means for catching fish from the Ozark streams, even without orthodox tackle. The spear, snare, and contrived lures might all be effective. For such game as birds and small furbearers, which would be necessary to a good diet, more ingenuity would be required. Snares, deadfalls, and box traps might be used, or one might develop enough skill with homemade bow and arrow to bag his meat. The thing could be managed, at least for a short period; yet on the whole, we prefer to stick to our garden produce, milk from old Betsy, and an occasional steak from a fat steer that went into the locker last autumn.

A Helping Hand for Bees

In ordinary years, our Ozark autumn is one of the best seasons for the honeybees. It is a time of heavy honey flow, when nectar and pollen are produced by goldenrod and aster, blue lobelia and cardinal flower, and the yellow Spanish needles that the bees particularly like. A year such as the present one, however, is an exception to this rule and the honeybees have had slim picking. A good many hives are likely to be lost this winter because the honey reserve stored up during spring and summer has been consumed during recent weeks. And this is apt to be doubly true where beekeepers took off the surplus supers during midsummer, leaving the swarms without an extra supply of honey.

Our own observation hive on the back porch, which Forest Ranger Giff Adams made for us, has been especially interesting to watch during the past week. This hive consists of a single large frame of comb enclosed on each side with glass, which has covers, except when we remove them to watch the bees, of thin sheets of Masonite. The whole is fastened to the inside of one of the porch posts with a solid bracket, and a hole has been bored through the post with a half-inch auger so that the bees have access to the outdoors. In the little hive are a queen and, at top capacity, perhaps four thousand worker bees. There is not room in the single frame of comb to store extra honey, though the supply is sufficient in times of good honey flow to keep this small hive going.

Because we were busy, we have neglected to keep a close watch on the observation hive during the hot, dry weather of recent weeks. And we were shocked when we looked at it a few days ago to find that we had almost lost our bees. All of their stored honey was gone, many bees lay dead in the bottom of the hive, and the rest moved about listlessly over the empty comb as though they knew they were doomed. Not enough flowers were blooming within flying range to keep them supplied with food and they had even stopped trying to keep the hive cleared of dead bees. I was afraid the queen might have been lost, but a quick search revealed her still alive.

Since it is often necessary to feed an observation hive during winter months because of its limited storage capacity, we have an opening on top where we can stand a jar of sugar water. This is a mixture of a pound of sugar dissolved in a pint of hot water, then placed in a glass jar with a lid in which are punched a number of small holes. Placed upside down on the opening in the top of the hive, the jar drips sugar water very slowly down to the bees. We promptly fixed up such a jar for the observation hive and then watched as a few drops ran down the glass sides. Immediately it was discovered by the nearest bees. They licked it up and hurried to take the news to the rest of the hive. Soon a steady line was moving up to the food source, and within a matter of hours a new spirit of hope and activity had come over the entire swarm.

One of the first things that happened, as soon as the bees were filled up and had renewed their energy, was that the hive was put into tiptop shape. Several hundred dead bees were dragged out, one by one, through the small hive entrance onto the landing platform outside, then pushed overboard. There were so many of these that we soon had to sweep them away. Then the bottom of the hive was cleaned of the debris that had collected there. Next the workers began to fill the empty combs with nectar made from the sugar water, until now many cells are half full. And the bees are flying again, heading out across the valley to come back loaded with yellow pollen that formerly they had been too weak or too lethargic to gather.

It is easy now, with so few workers in the hive, to find the queen. She is a regal creature: slim, shiny, with a body much longer than that of the workers and small wings folded neatly along her back. Once she has been hatched and has made her mating flight, her life is spent entirely in the hive at the task of egglaying. And she is hard at this now, moving from cell to cell to deposit her eggs, which will hatch first into small white grubs that are fed by the young workers, and then into worker bees. These will take their turn at caring for the young in the hive before going out to make their exploratory flights and settling down to their short working life of about six weeks at gathering nectar and pollen. Some will fall prey to birds and dragonflies, but most will work away until their gossamerlike wings become ragged and, on some heavy-laden homeward flight, they are unable to reach the hive.

This is the destiny of the honeybee—and a somewhat sad one until we think of the tremendous productivity of the hive. Each worker gathers perhaps a teaspoonful of honey in its lifetime to contribute to a store that may, in a good season, amount to 150 pounds or more for the hive. The population of the hive during a good summer may run to sixty thousand or more bees and is kept at this level by the egglaying capacity of the queen. Few insects are more useful; for we harvest more than a quarter-million tons of honey annually in the U.S.A., in addition to ten million pounds of beeswax, and depend on the honeybee to pollinate millions of acres of fruit trees and legumes such as clover and alfalfa.

october

Blue Shadows Across the Hills

This is a month when it is a punishment to spend a single daylight hour indoors. October is the month of the deep, smoky, orange-colored harvest moon and of golden sunlight that sets the dust motes dancing in the clear air. It is a time of blue shadows across the painted hills. In early morning, dew-spangled spider webs deck every tree and shrub and even each blade of grass. And in the lazy afternoons, tiny young spiders venture to the tops of timothy stalks, there to spin the gossamer strands of silk that finally whisk them away in the soft breeze to go ballooning across the fields in search of new homes.

October is the month of wild harvest, which this autumn is as bountiful as any we can remember. Down along Saline Creek the vines of wild grape that climb the big trees are heavily laden with bunches of deep purple fruit. We have harvested a basketful or two of these to make wild-grape jelly, a wonderful accompaniment for venison and wild duck and broiled quail on toast. The hazelnuts are gone from our valley, but we have one bush planted in the yard that this season, for the first time, bore a heavy crop.

On any morning after a shower we can pick basketsful of meadow mushrooms in the fields or enough of the delicately flavored giant puffballs for several meals within a dozen steps of the front door. These two, along with morel of early spring, are the most easily recognized and generally eaten of all our mushrooms. The meadow mushroom is delicious when broiled with a good steak. But the puffballs are more substantial, and when peeled, sliced, and fried in butter can furnish the main course for a meal.

Now the weather is cool enough to enjoy riding. We have brought old Ribbon and Daisy in from the far pasture where they have run wild during much of the hot weather. Each morning we call them into their stalls for a small "bait" of oats so that they will gentle down. And when other tasks are not too pressing, we saddle the horses for a short round of the farm. These rides give us our best opportunity for looking over the fields and planning work to be done, as well as for checking the cattle. Just this morning we discovered a newborn calf with its mother, down in the east pasture. But the calf was up and going and had obviously fed, so we called to Tiger and left without disturbing it.

Generally our first real frost comes in early October to ripen the persimmons and hazelnuts. There was a day last week when Matt and I were plowing and the wind blew a half gale out of the southwest for hours. In late afternoon the temperature dropped; as we came in to put the tractors away and feed the livestock, Matt said, "There'll be frost tonight if the wind drops." Next morning we found the thermometer standing at 34° and the ground covered with white frosting that glistened as the sun topped Buford Mountain, but soon vanished as the day warmed up.

In October the mockingbird's song takes on a soft and somewhat reminiscent tone. Although the bird feeding trays are still empty, we notice that chickadees and titmice and Carolina wrens make daily inspection tours, while downy and hairy woodpeckers come looking for suet and peanut butter. But there is still a plentiful supply of food in the fields and woods, and even in the yard and garden close to the house. Giant sunflowers in the garden still hold some seed and pokeweed along the yard fence is bending over with the weight of its purple fruit. The buckthorn bushes bore a heavy crop and there are elderberry and wahoo, blackhaw and bittersweet, and all the dogwoods and many more. So we will wait awhile before setting out food for the songbirds.

On any morning when work takes us down about the Big Pond, we are sure to find a band of blue-winged teal resting and feeding in the shallows, or sometimes sleeping out on the bank with their heads tucked under their wings. These are our earliest waterfowl, but soon they will be followed by other varieties— ring-necks and scaups, gadwall, baldpate, pintail, shoveler, and last of all the mallard. How long our wild ducks stay depends on whether plentiful rainfall puts water in all the ponds and thus scatters the birds across their flyway. One thing we have missed in the dry years is our flight of woodcock and Wilson's snipe, which probably stick close to the big streams.

Not long ago, driving the back-country gravel roads in Carter County, we encountered four tarantulas in a stretch of some fifteen miles; all of them apparently were migrating to new territory, or were on the search for a mate, since autumn is the mating season for the species. One of these fellows was a monster with a body that must have measured two inches in length and a legspread of fully four inches.

Tarantulas are the giants of the spider world, although, contrary to common opinion, their bite is not poisonous. It can be painful, however, for they have a powerful set of jaws suitable for crushing the insects taken in their nocturnal hunting forays. During the day, except in mating season, they normally stay hidden under boulders or old logs. There are about forty members of this family and some of the largest ones in South America are probably capable of catching small birds. Their chief enemy is a family of wasps called tarantula hawks, big and handsome insects that attack the spiders by upsetting them, then paralyzing them with a sting, after which the wasps store the tarantulas away alive to serve as food for their young.

Although they look much alike, our tarantulas belong to a different family from those found in the neighborhood of Taranto, Italy, from which city they take their name. It is said that during the Middle Ages a strange form of hysterical malady was caused by this spider's bite. The disorder called tarantism was marked first by melancholy and then by an irresistible desire to dance—though this may have been a form of convulsion. At any rate the city, the spider, and the strange malady all helped name the lively, whirling Neapolitan dance called the tarantella.

This has been a strangely beautiful October, a season to remember for years to come, were it not that the land cries out for rain. Oftener than not, when we wake in the morning, we find that despite having left the doors or windows open the night before, there is hardly a hint of chill in the house. At this hour the sky above Buford Mountain to the east shows only the faintest sign of dawn. Down in the woods along the creek, the horned owl seems to be grumbling about some bit of bad luck in last night's hunting; it is difficult to say whether he is the earliest riser of the wild creatures or only the last to go to bed. When I step outdoors the stars are bright and I note Orion, the hunter, sweeping past overhead, about as far beyond the zenith, as Aldo Leopold once put it, as you would lead a teal.

Somehow, despite the drought, the hills take on their usual magnificent pattern of color, though we note that the slightest stirring of air brings down a rain of leaves. Trees stand out vividly in the morning light—yellow and scarlet of maple and the deeper tones of the sour gum and the oaks. By afternoon the thermometer rises into the high eighties and the landscape changes to a smoky gold that turns to lavender toward evening. All of the insects are enjoying the reprieve brought about by lack of a killing frost—the spiders and grasshoppers and crickets and katydids, which still sing through the dusk, although in a subdued key.

The Groundhog

There are advantages to living in a countryside that is a jumble of fields and woods, creeks and ponds, patches of waste ground and thickety fencerows. Land such as this supplies a variety of environments so that it supports a good population of birds and wild animals, both in number of individuals and range of species. These are our neighbors, and they have as good a right to live out their lives here as we have.

We have even made our peace with the groundhogs or woodchucks, which farmers generally regard as a nuisance and hunters as a target. These furry little fellows are great forage eaters, consuming a considerable amount of such crops as clover and alfalfa. Also they are tremendous diggers, so that their burrows are sometimes a danger to livestock. Yet the groundhog generally digs at the edge of the field and very often a few yards back in the wooded border. And here there can be little doubt that its excavating activities have a useful purpose, since the burrows serve as shelters and dens for other small furbearers and especially for the cottontail rabbit.

The groundhog—or woodchuck, as it is known in the eastern part of its wide range—is actually an engaging and peaceable little animal. It harms no other creature and, except for man and his dogs, has few enemies. It can, in a pinch, be eaten, although it seldom is hunted by man for this purpose. Its pelt, moreover, has little value, so that it is scorned by the trapper. Yet in spite of this and of the fact that it consumes almost any sort of plant food and thus seldom suffers from a limited diet, the groundhog population seldom gets out of hand.

We generally start watching for the groundhog in mid-April, when it awakens from its long winter's sleep and comes out looking for food. This is also its mating season and the young are born after just four weeks, generally about a half dozen of them in a litter. For several weeks they remain in the nest that the mother has built deep down in the burrow. But by alfalfa-cutting time, the youngsters are fat and fully furred out and can often be found playing and feeding around the mouth of the den.

Once the young are old enough to forage for themselves, the family breaks up and each one is on its own. For groundhogs are actually solitary creatures, each having its bit of territory and its own burrows. These burrows are remarkable structures, often going down for six feet, then extending laterally for twenty-five feet or even more. There is a mound of dirt around the main entrance and then, four or five feet down the slanting tunnel, a sort of barricade of dirt that blocks off any direct view of the depths and also probably serves as a sort of observation post for the owner. Somewhere far from the entrance the groundhog digs a side tunnel ending in a sort of room where it sleeps and stores emergency rations. And somewhere far from the main entrance, which is marked by the inevitable dirt mound, the groundhog digs straight upward until it comes out above ground again. This gives it an emergency entrance, well hidden in the grass and inconspicuous because there is no telltale pile of dirt to mark it.

During the summer a groundhog may dig several dens. One will be out in the field where the forage is heaviest, another at the edge of a cornfield, and still another close to a creek or spring. Or one of the burrows may be quite deep in the woods. This afternoon I came upon a fat young groundhog stretched out in the sunlight at the base of a big oak tree. Since the dogs weren't with me, I could sit down close by and watch. The youngster yawned and stretched, dozed awhile, awakened to scratch its ear with a furry forepaw. Finally, when I tossed a small clod of dirt, it gave a sharp, flutelike whistle and dove into its burrow among the roots.

As summer wears along, the young groundhogs mature and the old ones grow fat as senators. Often in early morning and late afternoon we see them standing contemplatively beside the mouths of their burrows, observing their small world with a calm and philosophical eye. Summer has been good and all during early autumn they've been storing fat for the long winter's sleep that lies ahead. I suppose the largest groundhog is seldom more than twenty-four inches in length and with a weight of perhaps twelve pounds. But at this season, when we see one of the big fellows waddling sedately across the alfalfa field, it would be easy to guess he would tip the scales at twice that figure.

As the days grow shorter and a chill comes to the morning air, the groundhog becomes less active. Now we see it mostly in the afternoon when the October sun has warmed the air. And each night its sleep becomes deeper and each day its blood circulates more slowly and its awakening is later. Finally, as the leaves fall and most mornings bring sharp frost, there comes a day when it does not waken at all. Gradually its pulse slows until, from eighty beats a minute, it slows to a mere dozen. Curled deep in its den, its normal 95° temperature gradually drops to 40°. If we could watch, its breathing would be almost imperceptible, coming only a dozen times in an hour. Thus our small and furry companion of the summer meadows has rounded out the cycle of its active year and we will see it no more until the April sun warms the earth again and sets the meadow to growing.

Insects' Last Stand

We are especially conscious, during the lazy golden days of late October, of the insects making their last stand before hard frost and cold weather. Butterflies of many kinds drift through the soft sunlight, visiting the flowers that have taken a new lease on life with the coming of cool nights. Yellowstriped garden spiders of unusual size spin their webs, which each morning are bespangled with dewdrops. Caterpillars are active, eating their fill before taking to winter quarters, some hibernating under leaves and in brush piles, others spinning their cocoons to spend the cold months in the pupal state.

October is the time when the beautiful monarch butterflies gather for their southward migration. The monarchs are milkweed butterflies, and the only members of this small family in the Midwest. They use the various milkweeds both as food plants and for laying their eggs, and it is on these plants that we find the pale-greenish yellow caterpillar of this species. The monarch is also the main migrant among all our fragile-winged butterflies. The big brown insects congregate in large numbers for their long flight, and now and then in autumn you may find a tree actually weighted down with them. Many fly a thousand miles or more to reach the southern boundaries of the United States, the West Indies, or Central and South America, where they hibernate. In spring at least some of them fly northward again to lay their eggs on the milkweed plants.

One of the nymphalid butterflies, the viceroy, so closely resembles the monarch that it might be called "mimic adaptation." The monarch, for some reason, is highly unpalatable to birds, while the viceroy is evidently considered a delectable tidbit. Thus it seems that if the birds confuse the two by sight, the coloration may serve as a protection.

Another beautiful family of butterflies are the swallowtails

—all of them large and brilliantly colored, and the various species ranging over the continent as far north as the Arctic Circle. Here in the Midwest our swallowtails seem especially attracted by the orange butterfly weed, and by the thistles and ripe fruit in the orchard.

The colors in the wings of butterflies and moths may be of pigment or may be structural. In the latter case they are caused by light falling onto tiny parallel ridges in the wing structure or onto a very thin transparent film that breaks it into its components like the surface of a soap bubble. Butterflies are day flyers, while most of the moths are nocturnal. Both have long antennae, but those of the butterflies are smooth and filamentlike with a knob at the end, while those of the moths are generally feathery or constructed like the leaf of a fern. The tongues, or proboscises, of both moths and butterflies, which may be adapted to special flowers, are actually tubes that coil up beneath the head like a watch spring.

Not long ago, out beneath a zinnia bed that recent showers had brought to life, we noticed many butterfly wings. A little search disclosed a large mantid or praying mantis living in the nearby hedge. But since this is a valuable caterpillar-eating insect —and since all too many of the butterflies lay eggs that hatch into vegetable-eating caterpillars—we are glad to have the mantid. They are strangely intelligent-looking creatures and we have found them this summer in sizes from newly hatched youngsters not more than a quarter-inch long to big fellows that measure four inches. They change color from light green to dark gray, depending on whether their hunting ground is green foliage or gray bark. They also seem to have two sets of eyes, a large pair of prominent "compound" eyes and three small "simple" eyes set in a triangle above the others. The mantids are slow-moving, but good hunters, staying still as a twig until some unsuspecting insect comes in range, then grasping it swiftly with their strong forelegs. A single mantid can often be kept as a pet for weeks. But if two are put in a cage together, one will soon be eaten by the other, and, like some spiders, the female often consumes the male after mating.

Shore Birds Head South

A good many years ago, the late Clark McAdams, editor of the St. Louis *Post-Dispatch*, penned a verse that has always seemed to me the epitome of autumn as it is seen by the outdoorsman:

> A plover flying by with his plaintive call—
> The first wee prophet of the Fall,
> Leading his swift and fledgling band
> Out of the north land . . .

The lines were recalled to me on a recent Saturday afternoon when I spent a lazy sunny hour beside a neighbor's pond, watching the shore birds congregating for their long and uncharted flight to the south. The sight is an unusual one for our high upland prairie, set amidst the Ozark hills. But this pond is large, and very low from the drought, so that it presents an extensive mud flat around the shore line. The plovers and sandpipers seem to find such places instinctively, for they come circling in from considerable heights and drop down to stand teetering in the shallow water.

I had gone to the pond in the hour before sunset especially to watch them, and made myself comfortable under a walnut tree, some fifty yards from the bank, before unstrapping the binoculars to see what species I could identify. The sun at my back cast a long shadow and had lost the intensity of midafternoon, and over beyond the pond a field of ripening corn made the autumn scene complete. Soon above this cornfield, hundreds of swallows were darting and dipping, pausing now and then to perch in long rows on the wires of the power line. I could identify the steely blue and white of the tree swallow, the reddish breasts of barn swallows, and the brown and white markings of bank swallows. Now and then, with a sharp clicking of wings, they would circle in and drop down to drink from the pond. It seemed evident that, in company with the shore birds, they were gathering for migration.

Flying at every height above the field and pond were a hundred or more nighthawks or bull bats, often called mosquito hawks. These are, of course, not hawks at all, or bats. They are flycatchers—and extremely useful ones—belonging to the order of goatsuckers and closely related to the whippoorwill. The scientific name of the bird is taken from one of its most interesting characteristics. Flying high in the air with its odd, erratic wing beat, the nighthawk will suddenly fold its wings and plunge earthward in a perpendicular dive. Just above the ground, the dive is checked and the impact of air on the taut wings makes a loud sound as though someone had struck a deep chord on a bass viol. Thus the scientific name *Chordeiles* comes from the Greek words *chorde*, a stringed instrument, and *deile*, meaning evening, which is when the bird is generally seen.

Doves come to the pond in pairs and groups of a half dozen, rocketing in on swift wings, alighting on the flats to drink, and then taking off again. Coming to drink at sundown is characteristic of these beautiful birds and is a habit that makes them fairly easy prey for the sportsman. The young birds especially fly in without caution, and they are not as fast as the older ones. Many bird lovers feel that the mourning dove should be placed on the songbird list; yet their numbers seem to hold up remarkably well in the face of a short hunting season, and it is possible that other environmental factors might limit their numbers if we stopped hunting them.

With the coming of fall rains, the countryside in our valley seems to take a new lease on life. Bluegrass that remained dormant all during the hot, dry months has started growing and the pastures are greening up as if it were spring. Even the annuals in the flower garden and Ginnie's rose bed are putting forth their most luxurious blossoms of the season, while purple asters brighten the country roadsides. Livestock farmers are

hoping for a spell of Indian summer with mild nights and no killing frost, so that our fields will furnish a few more weeks of grazing for the cattle. In a year of drought when forage crops and grain are scarce, this would be a big help. But the nights are already growing cold and on two mornings recently we have found the thermometer at freezing and the fields white with frost.

Over the week end, Myron and Muriel Northrop stopped for a day and night on their way home to Little Rock, and Marge and Jimmy Nordman, who were heading for Norfork Lake, spent Saturday night. In the morning we hiked out along the ridge to check on the cattle and found the fields covered with a bountiful crop of white and tender mushrooms, a dividend from the recent showers.

A companion on our walk was the latest kitten, a handsome little gray tommie which I heard crying outside the door on one of the first cold nights. He was not at the door, in fact, but high up in one of the big sugar maples, with Tiger sitting expectantly beneath him with his mouth wide open, waiting for the kitten to drop. Too softhearted to let the little fellow go hungry, we coaxed it down and fed it warm milk and some of the dog's ration—fare that old Veronica scorns. One meal is all that is needed to make a fast friend of a hungry kitten, so we have a new boarder, though it will have to pay its way by sleeping in the granary and catching mice.

On our walk, the kitten made a hundred small exploratory side excursions, chasing grasshoppers in the field and digging for crickets in the woods. Now and then, when Tiger decided it was time for a chase, I would have to rescue it from the top of a tree; and when I carried it across the creek, it clung to my shoulder in fright. But this soon passes and now, instead of arching its back and hissing when Tiger comes near, it curls up between his paws and goes to sleep. The pup is a natural retriever, and this morning I was not surprised to see him marching around the yard with the kitten dangling unconcernedly from his mouth.

november

Late Autumn Days

All last week the days grew warmer and, though we know such weather can not last, we make the most of it. There are endless tasks to get the farm ready for winter and we are thankful we don't have to carry them out in rain and snow. Machinery that won't be needed until spring is carefully checked and stored away, while tools that we may use for cold-weather jobs are moved out to where they can be easily reached. We are building new pens and a shed for the young registered bulls, making the feed bunks ready, and repairing the calf creep at the barn. Here our calves will come in to eat extra grain and hay where they aren't in competition with the mature cattle. The daily round of feeding has started, a task that requires a couple of hours each day, although we are still hauling hay out to scatter on the ground in the fields and won't bring in the herd until bad weather really starts.

On one of these cloudy late afternoons with a spray of mist in the air I had taken hay to the cattle in the bottom field and then turned the dogs out for a run. Suddenly far off to northwest I heard the unmistakable calling of wild geese, and soon a great band of them appeared above the mountain, flying just below the scud of clouds. There were several hundred in long, wavering V's; and before they were out of sight and hearing, another band appeared—and then still another. For more than an hour the flight continued, until more than two thousand must have passed. Most of the flocks were moving at cloud level, but some were so low that I could distinguish Canadas, blue, snow geese, and the brownish-gray white-fronted geese.

It is to me thrilling to watch these beautiful travelers of the skyways and listen to their wild, somehow disconsolate calling. And I fell to wondering how many centuries they had migrated across our valley, so far from any large waterway. Perhaps their ancestors were here aeons ago when our Ozark country was a level plain and covered by successive inundations of an inland sea. For these hills comprise perhaps the oldest land area on our continent; from the varying limestone deposits, the geologists trace at least five of these inundations during the slow passage of countless centuries, and there were probably several more.

The vast ranges of the Rockies are actually "young" mountains in comparison with our small and rugged Ozark hills, which were pushing up out of the level plain perhaps a half-billion years ago. When these mountains were originally formed, they rose to elevations of five thousand feet or higher. But erosion and weather action through the milleniums have carved them into gentler shapes, gradually carrying away the softer rock until—as in the St. Francois hills that surround our Belleview Valley—only the bare granite and porphyry remain.

In this first Ozark uplift and in later upheavals that occurred, the limestone layers were faulted and carved with the channels of many streams. Water seeping down through the faults carried enough organic matter in suspension to make mild acids, which in time dissolved the soluble rock to create underground streams. Whenever a surface stream, in its constant

process of cutting a deeper channel, crossed an underground
stream, a spring was born.

As might be expected in a land so ancient, the soils of the
Ozarks before the area was despoiled by the white man were
exceedingly complex—and so were the life forms that the
region supported. Although some of them are extinct today, it
was not long ago that the Ozarks could boast some two thousand
species of plants and no fewer than seven hundred kinds of
animals, birds, fishes, reptiles, and amphibians. This may well
have set the record for any area of similar size on our continent.

In the old records the earliest travelers tell of parklike
forests of big widely spaced trees with many grassy openings
and small upland prairies where the tall Indian grass and big
bluestem held sway. Through the forest, even in the time of
these earliest white men, moved herds of buffalo and elk as well
as deer. Wild turkey abounded and the clear streams running
through untouched forests teemed with game fish. Early settlers
found life as easy as life can ever be on a frontier—with good
hunting, a wide variety of game, easy grazing for their livestock,
and foraging for their hogs. This land of abundance is in sharp
contrast to the Ozarks we have known, which went through
years of misuse that led to poverty and are only now beginning
the long, uphill climb to restoration and productivity.

Country Station

Last week end on a gray day we drove down to Carter
County and, on the way home, stopped at Ironton to put my
sister Helen aboard the train for St. Louis. The small but at-
tractive station, neatly planted around the outside with evergreen
shrubs and warm and brightly lighted on the inside, sent my
mind traveling back to winter nights and country railroad stations of my boyhood. So, for that matter, did the streamlined
passenger train with its great twin Diesel engines that presently

came roaring around the curve with deep-voiced siren and oscillating headlight.

The country railroad stations I recall were small wooden buildings, bare of any ornament except for the sign under the gable at each end announcing the name of the town. These stations were always painted on the outside in a combination of drab yellow and bilious brown. Inside, during winter weather, was a cannonball stove fired with lumps of soft coal that sometimes smoked and left the room with little oxygen. This stove barely kept from freezing the passengers condemned to catch early-morning trains, managed to be fairly comfortable by noon, and heated the room to the temperature of a moderate oven by evening. Kerosene lamps swung in ornamental iron brackets provided a dim illumination, enough to count your change at the station master's window, but seldom enough to read by if the train happened to be late. The only decoration in the waiting room, aside from the hard benches, was one fly-specked poster and a machine that vended chewing gum so old it crumbled to sawdust in the mouth.

Outside on the station platform was a high-wheeled baggage truck loaded with milk cans and other boxes and crates consigned to distant and mysterious destinations. As for milk cans, getting milk to town in those days was a slow and tedious process compared with today's methods. It was a process that began for the farmer many hours before daylight on a winter morning, first the milking in the dimly lit barn and then hitching the team to sled or light wagon for the trip to town. Nowadays the milk may flow from cow to milking machine and through glass tubes to the cooling tanks, whence it is pumped through more tubes into the glass-lined and refrigerated truck that hauls it to the city without its ever having been exposed to the air or any possible source of contamination.

The train in those far-off days—or at least the one I remember best—was even more different from its modern-day counterpart than the station. This particular train operated on the four-mile branch line between Mineral Point on the main line of the old Iron Mountain to Potosi. It had a small engine with a high smokestack and I can recall that its crew kept that engine polished to perfection. Since they spent far more time sitting in their terminal stations than they did en route, there was plenty of time for engine polishing. The engineer was Mr. Woods and the fireman was Mr. Swift, and, as far as I can remember, no one ever left off the "Mister" in addressing them. We were still close enough to the age of the horse—in fact, we lived in the very middle of it—so that the drivers of this coal-eating, smoke-snorting monster were spoken to with respect.

The rest of the train seldom varied, unless there happened to be an extra freight-car load of railroad ties or a gondola of "tiff" or a box car of wheat heading over to the main line. Otherwise there was one car in which passengers rode, though half of this was devoted to mail and baggage. The car also sported a cannonball stove, a couple of big brass spittoons, and a pair of coal-oil lamps that swung wildly in their brackets as the train rocked along over its four miles of curving and none-too-level roadbed. Since the passenger car was often right behind the engine and never more than a car or two away it received a continuous shower of cinders from the smokestack. In winter the windows were kept hermetically sealed and the interior of the car developed a truly remarkable bouquet. It was made up of a combination of liberal parts of coal smoke, strong pipe and chewing tobacco, the felt overshoes of farmers, the wool jackets of lumber workers, which steamed on wet nights, and numerous lesser items.

At the Potosi end of the line, the livery-stable hack would be waiting to take the mail and a traveling drummer or two up-town. There might also be a farm wagon or two, especially if it was a week end, to pick up the teacher coming home from her school in a neighboring town or some visitor from the city. Generally the livery hack had plenty of room for me to ride the half mile to Grandpa Hall's house, especially since the driver was a friend of mine. This particular fellow was hardly an ornament to the town. He was small and ugly, with a fine great pair of handlebar mustaches that he had developed in some Western cow town. His language was picturesque in the extreme and of a quality to curl the hair of the most recalcitrant horse or mule. He was a good hand with stock, a skillful driver, and, in my eyes, considerable of a daredevil. On Saturday nights he would sometimes load up on redeye—though where he got it was a mystery to Grandpa Hall who led the militant dry forces of the village. On these occasions, the hack driver would saddle the meanest horse in the livery stable and gallop down Main Street, unloading his trusty thirty-eight into the wintry sky. It made a wonderful racket and gave the respectable townsfolk something to be shocked about. It also gave Brother Anderson of the Prebyterian Church the subject matter for some of his most tempestuous sermons.

Time for Reflection

Coming home from an Ozark jaunt the other afternoon, it occurred to me again how hard it is, in this modern world, to find time for reflection, for ordered thinking. Perhaps the age we live in is against us—the monotony or extreme tension of the daily task, the bombardment of our senses by a thousand distractions, the strange belief that only through amusement can we secure relaxation, even the state of world stress and uncertainty. The printing press, the air waves, the image on the silver screen—these instruments to fill our leisure rob us of this most precious possession.

We think of the mind as a highly valuable part of our

being, a storehouse for knowledge, fact, information, and even wisdom. We conceive it as a smoothly functioning machine, capable of solving for us most of the problems of living. Yet we are amazingly unselective in the material we store away in this warehouse and the way in which we use it. Inside, the mind is apt to resemble nothing so much as a housewife's handbag in a state of hopeless confusion. Turn it upside down and shake it; out falls a remarkable jumble of information and misinformation, all cluttered together, a tangle of fact and fiction, tolerance and prejudice, and countless odds and ends.

If there is any purpose to this catchbag of thought and image that we call the mind, it must be to capture for each one of us some sense of the reason for being; since without this, life becomes empty of meaning and sinks to the level of the lowest animals. Yet it is not necessary that this "reason for being" be the same for all people or, indeed, for any two of us. Thus St. Francis of Assisi had as his all-impelling reason for being, if we may judge from *The Little Flowers,* the salvation of the human soul. In the same way this reason may be, for the poet, the translation of visual beauty or some noble idea into the imagery of words. For the builder, it is the creation of the towering skyscraper or far-flung bridge that spans the mighty river; or for the statesman, the molding of a better world for mankind.

Even for those of us who are neither saint, poet, nor statesman, there must be fairly well-defined reasons for being if life is to have form and meaning. Food, clothing, the daily tasks at office, factory, farm, or in running a home; good companions, travel, amusement—all these are necessary and a part of living. Yet if they are the only images that fill our minds, we are living at about the level of a contented cow or a well-fed hunting dog that asks no more of life than a day in the field with his master and a warm place beside the fire.

Fortunately for the human race, however, few minds are satisfied with only the images relating to physical comfort. We find something outside ourselves in which we become interested. This interest cannot develop without thought, concentration, reflection, and the accumulation and orderly filing away in the mind of information. The farther we pursue the interest, the broader it becomes; and as it develops, it adds constantly to our sense of the meaning of life. Most children who have the opportunity become interested in the outdoors; but here and there is one who develops a special curiosity about plants, birds, animals, or the very stuff of which the earth is formed. From among these come our naturalists, biologists, geologists, foresters, agricultural scientists. The hunter becomes curious about the conditions under which his quarry lives and eventually becomes a conservationist. The nature lover becomes a defender of the wilderness, and the amateur ornithologist finds himself involved in the relationship of man to his whole physical environment.

There is no field, it seems to me, that offers more opportunity for the enrichment of human life than the natural world all around us. Many of us, it is true, have lost our roots in the land. We live in cities and towns where it is easy to forget our dependence on the world of soil, water, sun, plants, and animals. We view with complacency the attitude of expediency and "enlightened self-interest" toward these resources on which our very existence depends. We are not disturbed that men treat the crop and forest lands, the marshes and grassy plains, as property in the purely economic sense, to be used and exploited according to the whims of the individuals who happen to claim ownership at some given moment.

There is a fallacy in this belief that economics must determine our whole attitude toward the land. Time and again individual landowners discover through the investment of time, skill, forethought, and faith that their land is not an enemy to be conquered, but a partner in a continuing adventure in rich and satisfactory living.

First Quail Hunt

As I write this, Mike dreams beside the fire, a tired old Irish setter, though hardly more so than his master. Now and then he whimpers softly in his sleep, his gray muzzle quivers, and his feet move as though he were running. Close beside him lies young Tiger, not nearly as tired as Mike or I, for he keeps one ear cocked in our direction and comes over to have his head scratched. Yet he seems glad enough for a quiet evening, and it is no wonder, for this was opening day of the quail season.

An intelligent bird dog seems to sense unfailingly the approach of this most important of all days in a bird dog's existence. All autumn, from the time cool weather started, Mike and Tiger have ranged the fields with us whenever we are abroad about the farm. Whether we're hiking or working with the tractor or riding the mares, the dogs sweep ahead of us and point when they find birds. But Mike, at least, knows this isn't serious business—and Tiger will also know, by the time another season rolls around. In fact, when I'm out in the fields with the tractor, Mike will make his swing and then head across the fields at a lope for home.

When opening day arrives, all playfulness and indifference are over for Mike, though it may take the young dog a couple of hunts to settle down. Both of them, however, look with interest at the twenty-gauge, now taken down from the gun rack and standing in the corner of the kitchen. Ran Barrett of the Conservation Commission has come to open the season with us, as usual, arriving the evening beforehand so that we can make an early start. He brings his duffle bag, boots, and gun, depositing them in the front hall where both dogs sniff them with an air of satisfaction. We have our before-dinner toddy in front of the fire. The old dog stretches in the middle of the rug, head on crossed paws, never taking his eyes from us. Unlike Tiger—and unlike himself on ordinary occasions—he doesn't beg for affection. The season and the task for which he was born and for which he lives forty-two weeks out of every year are at hand.

This year we made our opening hunt on Armistice Day. The morning came clear as a bell, cold, and without wind. Frost lay white across the valley, but it would thaw later on to make an ideal day afield. Moisture would linger in the vegetation to help hold bird scent. The sun came up over Buford, I hurried out to do the chores, and then we took our time tucking away Ginnie's fried apples and sausage. There was even time for a third cup of coffee, since the birds would not move out from their roosts to feed until the sun had touched the frost.

With the whole day ahead of us, I decided we would make our start away up at the east boundary of the farm and hunt down to the creek by noon. This would cover the larger share of the territory, because I have found that in recent years we no longer take in as much ground as we used to after a good noon dinner. There was a time when one thick sandwich of cold country sausage, an apple, and a drink of spring water—each shared with the setter—were all a fellow needed to keep going hard from early morning until dusk. This would still suit Tiger, but Ran and Mike and I are older; and though there has been no slackening of Mike's pace, we ease things down by shortening the length of the day afield.

The first covey was right where it "belonged to be," as the mountain people put it, in a patch of long grass and lespedeza among some cedars, no more than fifty yards from the precipitous, brushy shelter of Buford Mountain. Both dogs were quartering the field when Mike made game, then came down on a solid point—and I was proud of the way Tiger backed. The dogs were between the birds and the mountain, but we learned long ago that quail fly toward their natural cover, no matter how hard you try to turn them. We walked in, took two on the rise, and failed, as one nearly always does at the beginning of the season, to mark down the scattered covey. But I'd watched them flare to clear the oaks at the timber's edge and knew that what singles we found would be in heavy brush and halfway to the crest of the mountain. We followed them and Tiger found one, then overran another, and this was the last we saw of that covey.

The young dog found the next covey, however, only a few hundred yards away, at the edge of a blackberry thicket where a swale of heavy grass drains down into a small pond. This is an area that, next season, will be fenced off as wildlife cover with a hedge of multiflora rose and then planted to quail food. The covey was a big one, perhaps a dozen mature birds from last year and a well-grown hatch of this year's youngsters. On the rise, the whole covey headed for an open-woods pasture and here we were afforded the pleasure of some fine work on singles by both dogs. Before we had hunted these out, Mike was hard down on another covey, close beside Saline Creek.

When it was time to go again after lunch, the clock showed nearly three. But there were only a couple of birds needed to make up our Possum Trot limit of five per gun. Now the wild-life patches to the west of the house proved productive and we were back long before sunset with our quota filled. As always, Ran made careful examination of the crops while he cleaned the birds to find what foods they were using, and I hurried out to do the evening chores. The count didn't vary much from other hunts and other years: the little ragweed, Korean lespedeza, bits of corn and soybean from Stan Turner's field, and pin-oak acorns. A good variety and plenty of it, at any rate.

Deer Crossing

We think of the forest as a silent place. Yet it is more often than not filled with sound, as you would agree if you went out before daylight on a cold November morning to stand on a deer crossing. The particular place I had selected was an old sawmill clearing deep in the timber. A sawdust pile perhaps twenty feet high made a good observation post, surrounded by an opening of perhaps an acre in the forest with several old logging trails running into it. The location was at the head of a hollow with a spring branch running down it; in the opening grew many of the native legumes of the Ozarks, along with huckleberry, goldenrod, asters, and other plants on which deer like to browse.

Examination a few days before the season showed many deer were using this part of the forest. But on opening day, the sudden cold snap sent the deer to hiding in the thickest brush on the south hillsides. Here they are safe as long as they stay put. Few hunters have the stamina to beat out these tangled sides of the deep hollows and seldom get a shot when they do, for the leaves are still on and the visibility in the woods is nearly zero. So there were almost no deer taken in a big section surrounding our hunting ground on opening day, though we knew the deer were there.

There's something eerie about hiking an old woods road in the dark hour before dawn. The flashlight casts a weak beam ahead and you must be careful not to get off on any side trails. The cold seems most intense at this hour and you wonder if you will "freeze out" before sunrise. But in this case I planned to burrow a foxhole in the sawdust pile, knowing it would be fairly warm below frost line. So even at 18°, which the thermometer had read when we left at four-thirty in the morning, I managed to stay comfortable. The heaviest of long-handled "woolies," a pair of fleece-lined flyer's breeches, sweaters, wool shirt, and red jacket made it difficult to move but kept me from freezing.

No sooner had I settled in than I began to be conscious of sounds in the woods around me. The slightest breath of air set the tops of the pine trees to singing. But in long intervals when no breeze stirred, it was interesting to interpret other sounds. Far up on the hill above me, it sounded as though a deer might be browsing slowly along. Now and then an acorn would fall with a surprising clatter. Even a handful of dry leaves, detaching themselves from their twig and drifting in slow descent to the ground, made a noise that could be heard for a hundred yards in the stillness.

The first hint of dawn awakened the birds, of which there were more in the clearing than would be found in the dense timber. A chickadee spoke first, and then came the "tin horn" note of the nuthatch. Woodpeckers hammered away at the dead trees, each stopping now and then to sound its characteristic note. At daylight a pair of chipmunks came out of the slab pile and set up a great chattering—though not at my being there, for they couldn't see me. A fox squirrel jumped in a distant hickory tree, sending me instantly on the alert. A little later, as the sun climbed above the trees and shone down into my clearing, the squirrels came out to gather seeds. At one time I could count a half-dozen big pileated woodpeckers calling from different parts of the forest, and their loud "c-a-a-k, c-a-a-a-k, c-a-a-a-k," fairly set the woods to ringing. An hour after sunrise one of the big fellows lit in a dead snag, not thirty feet from my observation post.

It must have been ten o'clock when I dozed off for a few moments and woke with a start, afraid I might have let my chance come and go. There came a slight rustling from the draw on the far side of the clearing and a fawn stepped cautiously out of the undergrowth. It nibbled delicately at a stem of goldenrod and picked the leaves from a small low-growing vetch. But the little fellow couldn't have been long without the spots of fawnhood, and his weight of perhaps fifty pounds made him no target for the big thirty-forty Winchester. I guessed that his mother was probably off up the hollow flirting with some young buck, for this is the mating season of the white-tails. And I hoped that the buck with his harem might decide to come down through my clearing. In this I was disappointed.

Later in the morning, walking up the hollow, I found where the buck and two does had crossed the old road, and from the size of his track he might easily have been a ten-pointer. Not long after sunup there were a few shots away off to the south and east of my stand. But except for a single four-pointer taken up in the next hollow just after sunrise, no deer were bagged close by. At noon we met at the truck trail for a hot luncheon, then prospected some more good country a few miles away. But except for two deer we jumped out of a bunch of treetops on a steep hillside without ever seeing them, this country also proved unproductive.

On the afternoon of the second day I hunted alone down a long ridge above Current River, which splits Gooseneck Hollow into two prongs. This has been, in the past, good deer country and the day was ideal for still-hunting. The morning had brought high winds and a heavy rain that had left the forest floor saturated; a man could move through the thick cover of fallen leaves and undergrowth with almost no sound. There was still some wind, although as I worked down the lee side of the ridge it touched only the tops of the tallest oaks and pines.

I like this particular bit of woods because several years ago the Forest Service did some work to improve the stand, girdling the big cull timber that we call "wolf trees" and also taking out some saw logs. Now there is good deer food in the openings: sumac and huckleberry, Ozark rose, the big trefoil that we call beggar's lice or sticktight. Ordinarily the area contains lots of deer sign: scrapes on the young pines where bucks have rubbed the velvet from their antlers, indications of heavy browsing, and even tracks around rain pools in the old logging roads.

On this hunt I found almost no deer sign and finally followed the faint track of the logging road down a long point into the hollow. Here the wind was shut out entirely and the sun, which had stayed behind the clouds all day, began to break through. As far as I could tell, there were no other hunters in this whole area; at least, none nearer than the Eastwood road, some four miles away.

Finally, along toward four o'clock, I found a good spot in the hollow where several points ran down from the surrounding ridges and several dim trails came together. It seemed a likely location to finish out the afternoon, for it was not more than a mile from camp and at this time of day the deer are likely to move from the high ridges. They'll come drifting down a point, then move along an old woods trail on the way to their feeding ground for the night. But whether a deer appeared or not, it was a pleasant place to spend an hour on a November afternoon. The slanting sun brought all the color of the oaks on the opposite hillside into play, making a beautiful contrast to the vivid green of the pines. I had been on my stand for perhaps fifteen minutes when I heard the probable answer to the comparative scarcity of deer along Current River in Ripley County. Far up on the ridge to my north, on the side toward Spring Hollow, the hounds were running. And though it is illegal to run deer with hounds, they were making wonderful music. They came swiftly closer; finally, I heard a deer cross the ridge and go angling off to the west with the dogs behind. They went out of hearing up the hollow and were lost for a time; then I could hear the faint, belling echo made by the pack when it is too far away to distinguish individual voices. But soon they were distinct again, coming nearer, and I decided the deer was probably heading down my hollow to cross the river.

This looked like my chance for a buck and I made the Winchester ready and kept a sharp watch to westward. Then suddenly, with the hounds out of hearing again, I heard a rustle behind me and swung carefully around. Some thirty yards away a deer leaped into the road and stopped. It was a small doe that evidently had been hard pressed by the pack, for its tongue was out and its sides heaving. Yet it stopped to listen for its pursuers, as though to plan the strategy of its flight. Then it seemed to sense my presence, looked toward me for a moment, and was gone down the hollow like a ghost, with its white flag bobbing in the dimming light. I watched it go through the peep sight on the Winchester and somehow never thought of pulling back the hammer for what could only have been an easy shot.

Ten minutes later the hounds came up, their tongues out even farther than the doe's. I called them in and divided a good beef sandwich between them, and they seemed glad enough to lie at my feet awhile. They were local dogs, from the brass plates on their collars, and I expect run deer seven days a week— the best way to move all the deer out of a big piece of territory. Deer hunting is fun as it becomes a custom and a tradition with less and less emphasis on meat for the pot. This is the way at the Gooseneck Club, where we foregather each autumn during the deer season. There are Jerome Burford and T. L. and Joe Wright from Doniphan, who are owners and hosts, and much the same group of hunting companions. Jack Davis takes time off as town marshal to cook for us, and he turns out wonderful meals. Doc Stokely comes up from Poplar Bluff and there are Lin Edwards and Ran Barrett of the Conservation Commission and Bill and Tom Wright, who drive in forty miles from Doniphan for supper.

There was a time, years ago, when we would be sharply disappointed unless three or four bucks were hanging up by the second day of the season. Today the comradeship of the camp seems more important. We take a morning to go casting for jack salmon or sit on some bay in hope a bunch of mallards will drop in on us. And on the rainy morning, Doc Stokely and I watched the first of many thousands of ducks go over, far more than any of us had ever seen on Current River before. Of course we deer hunt, too, though there are generally more rifles in the rack at camp than there are on stands in the woods. But we will protect ourselves if attacked by a ten-point buck.

Some people feel deer hunting is an unwarranted sport. Yet the fact is that we can either have a deer season during which a fairly large proportion of the annual increase is harvested, and at the same time maintain a large and healthy deer herd, or we can go back to the situation that existed not so many years ago, when, with no deer season whatever, the white-tails were on the road to extinction. Most of us would, I believe, prefer to have 200,000 or more deer roaming the forests and prairies of our state with an annual hunting season than we would to have no hunting season and—eventually—no deer.

The reason why a plentiful supply of deer and a hunting season go naturally together is not hard to explain. People who spend their lives studying the ways of the wilderness know that the numbers of any wild bird or animal are chiefly controlled by three factors: the range that is available for each species and the amount of food and cover that this range provides. Other factors enter in: hunting pressure by man, predation by birds and animals that use this particular species for food, and the like. But the real keys to wildlife population lie in the over-all range, the food, and the cover.

This is as true of the white-tail deer in Missouri as it is of our bobwhite quail or, on a continent-wide scale, of wild waterfowl. When white men first came to settle west of the Mississippi, the area now embraced within the Missouri boundaries probably supported between 500,000 and 1,000,000 deer. These were widely distributed across the prairies, in woodlands along the water courses, and throughout the big timber country of the Ozarks. As more of this land was put to use, the range for the white-tails dwindled. First they disappeared from the prairie as these level grasslands went into cultivation. As human population multiplied along the rivers, the deer were driven from the small bits of woodland cover that remained. At last even the forested hills knew the deer herds no more as saw and ax harvested the virgin oak and pine, followed by clearing for mountain farms and burning and hard grazing of the cutover lands. By the end of the 1920's, deer had almost disappeared from the entire state, a condition that closed seasons seemed not to remedy at all.

What started the white-tails on the road back in Missouri was the growing interest in conservation. Early in the 1930's we established the Clark and Mark Twain National Forests in the Ozark counties, which put nearly two million acres of cutover land under good timber management for the first time. Fire was brought under control, grazing cut to a reasonable point, thousands of acres improved by removal of poor second growth and the girdling of old cull trees. In time, these rotted and fell to return humus to the forest floor and speed the growth of good young timber. Wherever this "release" work was done or where stands of usable timber were harvested for the sawmill, the openings thus created grew up in good deer-food plants that had formerly been starved out by second-growth scrub.

At the same time, Missouri created its nonpolitical Conservation Commission with responsibility for all the wild resources of the state. It also began a campaign for forest-fire control on private lands, better timber use, scientific wildlife management, and conservation education. Refuges were created where seed stocks of deer could multiply undisturbed; and when numbers had grown sufficiently, the Commission instituted a program of trapping and release of deer in suitable areas throughout the entire state. This program has been in effect for about twenty years, with the result that deer are seen today in every county in Missouri and are present in sufficient numbers in most counties to provide an open season.

The progress of the deer-restoration program is all the more remarkable when we recall that in the space of less than a hundred years deer numbers in Missouri had declined from perhaps 750,000, to 3,000 or even less. And the reopening of a hunting season for deer came about not merely because sportsmen wanted it, but because a substantial annual harvest soon became absolutely essential to the continued health of the herd. Ordinarily, under conditions of a bountiful food supply, about 50 per cent of does will drop twin fawns in a given year. This means that potentially the herd can double about every three years, so that 2,500 deer in 1936 could become 160,000 deer by 1954—and by 1957, 320,000 deer.

Under wilderness conditions, the herd is kept in check by natural predators such as the wolf and panther and by the changing pattern of weather, food, cover, and range. Thus it seldom gets out of hand. But when man steps in, the picture changes radically. All of the natural predators are wiped out and other conditions are controlled. The herd keeps growing until, literally, it explodes. Overnight there takes place what the wildlife men call a "population eruption" and suddenly the range, food, and cover are no longer sufficient to care for the numbers of deer. Then several unpleasant things happen, as experience in many states has taught us. The deer cannot spread out, because there is no range to spread into. Food supplies become insufficient and first the fawns and then the adult deer begin to starve. Often the food-plant species are so badly damaged they do not recover for years. The starved does become unthrifty and disease sweeps in to decimate the herd. Soon we are back to where we started and there are no deer.

In spite of all this, it seems to me that deer hunting tends to become an increasingly artificial sport, with less and less of skill and hardihood and knowledge of woodcraft required for its pursuit. As each season draws to a close, I find myself feeling glad that it is over—that now these beautiful dwellers of the forest can go back to the quiet and peace of their hills and hollows, safe for another year from all but the running dog pack, the occasional poacher, and the cars that drive too swiftly on highways that run through the deer woods.

WINTER

december

Winter Hills

December brings a special quality to the timbered Ozark hills that is to our liking. Some mornings are clear and frosty and still, so that the whole countryside is etched in sharp relief. Fields stretch away gray and brown, and beyond them the silhouettes of Buford and Round Hill, Belleview Mountain, and the ranges to westward rise in dark masses. Against these the cedars stand in black clumps and only the scattering pines and an occasional patch of wheat show bright green. At this season, with the foliage gone, the granite ribs of the land are laid bare, so that one gets the feel of its great age. In summer the green mantle of the forest softens the outlines of the landscape. In winter we are conscious of the countless centuries of erosion that have carved our ancient hills, leaching away the layers of limestone and sandstone that once overlaid the parent rock.

There are other mornings when a wind comes out of the south so wet you can feel it on your face; when low clouds race across the valley and obscure the crests of the ridges. And still other days when, at sunrise, the timber atop the mountains is covered with a heavy coating of white frost, though there is none on the lowlands. Altogether it is a good time of year, and only during times of cold rain or when an icy wind comes roaring down out of the northwest do we think with some longing of spring, which is months away. On such days the cattle keep to the cedar thickets, heads down and faces to the wind. In this they are unlike the horses, which drift along with their hindquarters to the gale. When I come in from feeding on these windy days there are icicles on my nose and ice on my cheeks from eyes that water steadily, for I have ridden the tractor across the fields for an hour.

Nowhere is the year's ending more clearly marked than in the trees. And few things in nature are more marvelous than the action of the cambium, that microscopically thin layer of living cells between wood and bark that completely envelops the trunk and every limb and branch without a break. During the growing season, the cambium cells carry the fluids that hold in solution the nourishment for the tree, this being necessary because the inner core of the trunk is inert and non-growing. When autumn comes, the cambium cells divide lengthwise, rearranging themselves with the new "daughter" cells outside the old cells. These latter now harden into a denser fiber to make the ring that marks the annual growth, while the new cells remain alive and ready to resume their food-carrying function when spring comes again.

Trees make their growth in spring and summer, and I recall August Bielmann at the Missouri Botanical Garden's Arboretum showing us how all the members of one species start out on about the same date and end their growth for the year at the same time, remaining dormant throughout the winter season. This is in contrast to many other plants. Our grasses, especially fescue and bluegrass, make some winter growth. Barley, rye, and wheat continue to grow throughout winter, stooling out from the first pair of frail shoots. Many biennials such as the mullein form a new rosette of leaves close to the ground that remains green all winter long. The trees and shrubs, although actual growth may be confined to spring and summer, are hard at work during this period making ready for the year ahead, forming the cells that will make next season's twigs, leaves, and flowers.

All these materials which will constitute next year's growth have been completely formed in miniature by the time autumn arrives. Tightly creased and folded and packed into tough, waterproof coverings, they will remain throughout cold weather in a state of suspended animation. These make up the winter buds that we see on trees and shrubs—or at least can see if we look sharply enough. Thus on the black haw in our yard the buds of the white flower clusters that will open next May are plainly visible, as are the buttonlike flower buds at the tips of dogwood branches. Also to be seen are other buds, those at the ends of branches containing next year's flower or twig, and others just above each leaf scar that contain the new leaf in miniature.

An interesting pastime when walking through the winter woods is to identify the deciduous trees now that the leaves have fallen. First there are broad characteristics, like the "witches'-brooms" in the hackberry or great patches of snow-white bark and hanging seed balls of the sycamore. Many smaller trees and shrubs, such as flowering dogwood, wahoo, possum haw or deciduous holly, black haw, and buckthorn, may be identified by their fruits or the conspicuous buds of next year. White oak is distinguished by its light gray bark and great arching branches, scarlet oak by the heavy growth of green lichens on the trunk. Burr oak grows a thick, sturdy trunk and heavy branches and generally has a goodly crop of mossy-cupped acorns that cannot be mistaken for any other. Sour gum sends its trunk straight upward with many small branches that grow out horizontally or with a slight droop.

There is a remarkable amount of color in the winter woods for the walker with an observant eye. Early in the season there are fruits of many species: brilliant red of dogwood, bittersweet, wahoo and possum haw, frosty blue of cedar berries, bright orange of wild-rose hips, purplish red of coralberry, and deep blue-black of buckthorn and black haw. Winter buds of the willow and red maple, twigs of young cottonwood and rough-leaved dogwood, the changing tones of the oaks, to which the leaves still cling. All these add to the interest and beauty of our Ozark winter.

Butchering Day

If you were raised in the country, few things will give you a more nostalgic feeling than the aroma of fresh pork sausage drifting from the kitchen on a cold winter morning. At the back of the stove, where there's no danger of burning, fried apples sweetened with brown sugar sizzle gently in a black skillet: while in the oven, biscuits rise and turn golden brown.

No product of the packer's art can possibly equal this home-seasoned delicacy, flavored to perfection with sage and just the right amount of other herbs. Nor for that matter can the tenderized and chemically treated ham compare with the best of those that are sugar-cured and hickory-smoked on the farm. It is equally true, however, that some of the paeans in praise of so-called country cured hams and bacon would be better left unsung. All too often these supposed delicacies turn out to be tough-fibered, salty, and with a gamy flavor that bespeaks improper curing.

For the best in hams, you need a hog that is a cross between the modern "bacon type" and the old-fashioned "lard type." Nor should its diet consist entirely of corn. A pig farrowed late in April will come up to butchering time in fine shape if care is taken in its feeding. Avoid hogs with very small pointed ears, since a keen sense of hearing is important, as will appear hereafter. Let the piglets run with the sows on good alfalfa pasture supplemented by a small amount of corn, tankage, and minerals during the summer months.

As autumn approaches, turn the litter of pigs out into a good woods pasture to harvest the crops provided by nature.

Now there are beans in the honey locust, rich in sugar and high in proteins to help impart flavor to the meat. With the coming of frost, fruits start dropping from oak and hickory and butternut, all of which are added to the diet. And this is where the keen ears come in, since the pig that can hear the acorn drop and catch it before it stops rolling gets plenty of exercise. Now the persimmons and papaws ripen and these too are eagerly gathered by the young porkers. Here are no flabby pigs, lolling away their days in the hog wallow and rising only to eat, but keen and healthy fellows adding flavor with each variety of food they take. Finally, bring the pigs in for a few weeks of concentrated feeding on yellow corn and skim milk; then keep your eye on the weather.

Butchering day at Possum Trot is a gala event. We try to pick a time when it is cool enough to chill out the carcasses properly, yet not so bitterly cold and windy that the work becomes an unpleasant chore. Everything is made ready the day beforehand; and since many hands make light work, we invite Harry Russell over to help Matt and me. With three of us on the job, our hogs are hung up by noon to chill, ready to be cut up next day. First of all a scaffold is rigged up, out in the shelter of the machine shed where we are protected from the wind. Close by, we back the wagon into position for a scraping table. With sideboards removed, it is just the right size and height. The scalding barrel is braced against the back wheel of the wagon and a big pile of wood is cut for the fires that heat the scalding water.

Two big black kettles on wrought-iron stands serve for heating the water, and these are brought out and made ready. Fortunately there's a spigot from the well close by, so we don't have to "pack our water from the spring branch," as was common in the old days. A tub of wood ashes is set handy to the scalding barrel so a few handfuls can be added to the water as needed. There is just enough lye in the ashes to help serve as a cleasing agent to remove the scurf, while it also seems to make the hair slip easier. The knives are sharpened to a fine edge and set out on the wagon bed, with a whetstone handy to keep them honed. Washtubs are scalded out and dishpans prepared to hold the hearts, livers, and other edible "innards" as the butchering goes forward.

We cure our hams and bacon sides in sweet brine, preferring this over the dry-salt method, and use big twenty-five-gallon masonry crocks for this purpose, so these are brought up from the cellar and thoroughly scalded. Salt, brown sugar, pepper, strained honey, and saltpeter are carefully measured for the brine mixture, the saltpeter being used to preserve the bright color of the meat. With everything ready, the butchering can proceed without any delays.

On the big morning we set the alarm a half hour early, to get breakfast out of the way. Then I hurry to fill the kettles and get the fires going while Matt feeds the cattle. At eight, Harry arrives in his pickup and the day's work begins. Half an hour later the carcasses have been brought from the pen and are ready for the scalding barrel. The important thing about this part of the job is to stick and bleed the hogs properly so there will be no blood in the carcasses.

The water in the kettles is bubbling merrily by this time. We bail out enough to fill the barrel, then refill the kettles with the hose so as to have a fresh supply when needed. A shovelful of ashes is tossed in and the water temperature tested; if too hot, it will cause the bristles to set. Harry's method is to run a hand through the water three times and if he doesn't get scalded, he says, "Just right." This seems to work perfectly, though a temperature of 150° is recommended if a thermometer is handy. Then into the barrel goes the first carcass, one man holding each hind leg and the two working in unison, dousing the hog up and down until a test shows that the hair slips easily. Then we reverse ends and follow the same procedure.

Once the carcass is out on the table, all hands fall to scraping away the bristles, now and then dipping a clean burlap sack into the hot water and using it to soak some spot where the hair doesn't slip easily. The scraping takes perhaps a half hour, when the first carcass is clean and white and ready to hang.

A slit is cut under the tendons above the hock in the hind legs, the gambrel stick is inserted into the slots, and the carcass hoisted to the scaffold. A clean tub is made ready for the "innards" and one of the workers with a steady hand and a sharp knife opens up the hog from top to bottom in one neat operation. Everything goes into the tub, which is then set aside for further attention. The head is removed by cutting clear around, just above the ears, then giving a sharp twist to sever it from the backbone. The carcass is now propped open with a clean stick cut for the purpose, sluiced out with cold water, and left to chill.

At ten-thirty comes an interval when Harry runs home to bring Ethel, who is coming to help Ginnie with lunch. Then fresh water goes into the scalding barrel and the second hog follows the first. Once it is hung to cool, there are the hearts and livers to clean and set aside, as well as other parts that will be cooked and frozen for Mike and Tiger and the cats. By the time this operation is completed, the ladies call us for dinner and the first day of butchering is over.

We like to chill out the carcasses overnight because it is then far easier to do a neat and professional job of trimming out the various cuts than while the meat is still warm. There are many good sources of information about cutting up and handling pork, a good one being the U. S. Department of Agriculture's Farmer's Bulletin No. 1186, *Pork on the Farm.* This gives instructions for killing, cutting up, curing and smoking, and also handling the various cuts that are used fresh. If these instructions are followed carefully, there is little excuse for the spoilage that each year still takes a heavy toll of farm-processed meat.

In our butchering we end up with hams, bacon sides, and shoulders to be sugar-cured, along with the jowls. Loins are cut into pork roasts for freezing, as we have found that these keep better than the thinner pork chops. Spareribs are also trimmed and wrapped for freezing, but the tenderloins are set aside to be eaten fresh. We used to grind our sausage at home and also render the lard in a big iron kettle over an outdoor fire. Today the locker plant with its power equipment can handle these chores so quickly and easily that we let them do the job. Lard is stored in five-pound buckets until needed. Sausage is left unseasoned, wrapped in packages of convenient size, and frozen, except for a few pounds we take home for immediate use.

There are good mixtures on the market for seasoning sausage; but we still prefer to mix our own salt, black and red pepper, rubbed sage, and a touch each of sugar, nutmeg, and mixed herbs. This mixture can be kept on hand, ready for each batch of sausage as it comes from the freezer. The recipe for curing the hams, shoulders, and bacon sides is also quite simple. For each 100 pounds of meat we mix eight pounds of table salt, three pounds of brown sugar, two tablespoons black pepper and one of red, and two ounces of saltpeter. This is dissolved in six gallons of water to which a cup of strained honey is added. The brine must be thoroughly mixed and the meat, when placed in the crockery jars, must be weighted so the solution will cover it completely.

One problem in home curing is to maintain a fairly even temperature throughout the process. This we accomplish by setting the jars on an enclosed porch where the thermometer stays at about 40°, which is ideal. Mold that forms on top of the brine can be skimmed off, but if the mixture becomes stringy, the meat must be removed, scrubbed thoroughly, and placed in a fresh solution. Hams cure at the rate of four days per pound, shoulders in three days, and bacon sides in two days. That means sixty days for a fifteen-pound ham, fourteen days for a seven-pound bacon side.

As the curing process is completed, the cuts of meats are

drained thoroughly and are ready for smoking. Four or five days in the hickory smoke give a nice mild-flavored bacon. Hams and shoulders, however, we like to smoke slowly for a full three weeks. This dries the meat thoroughly and helps ensure keeping quality after the hams are wrapped and hung to age.

Our smokehouse, which works well for the amount of meat we cure, is no more than a large iron barrel upended over the chimney of an outdoor fireplace. The meat is suspended from a rod thrust through the top of the barrel, which also has a small hole punched in it to let the smoke drift slowly through. The fire of hickory wood is built well out at the mouth of the fireplace so that the barrel temperature doesn't rise above 90°, and is kept well smothered with hickory sawdust. A little apple wood and a few corncobs can be added to the fire from time to time.

There are many farmers—perhaps the majority, in fact—who feel that home-curing their own meat doesn't pay. If done carelessly with a good part of the meat lost, it certainly does not. Yet we have had excellent luck during our ten years, and I expect that Possum Trot will go right on enjoying its own sugar-cured hams and bacon, tender pork roasts, and wonderful sage-flavored sausage on winter mornings.

Ice Storm

Over last week end the first real storm of winter blew in. Certainly nothing like the forty-below-zero weather reported from Montana or even the heavy snows in Colorado, but enough to let us know we live in the country. The thermometer began to drop early on Saturday morning and hard showers of rain came driving down, so that we had to slip out between spells to feed the heifers on the ridge near the barn and the cows over across the highway. We weren't too concerned for the cows, even if bad weather came, because no calves are due and the animals have good shelter in the heavy thicket of cedars. And there's nothing a husky Hereford minds less than rough weather.

Along about noon, however, the thermometer dropped to freezing and the rain kept coming down, with now and then a touch of sleet. All afternoon it kept up and we could see the thick coating of ice forming on the trees and multiflora hedges and even on the grass in the fields. About four o'clock, just as

I started out to finish the feeding while it was still daylight, we heard a tremendous crash and the lights went out. Looking up toward the old elm tree that stands on the road near the barn, we saw that at least one huge hollow limb had broken and tumbled down across the power and phone lines, flattening them both to the ground.

Generally when there is a power failure we report it by telephone and it is fixed in short order. This time there was no phone. So I hurried through the feeding, piled the woodbox full of logs for the fireplace and smaller wood for the kitchen stove, and then stacked extra logs—the biggest in the wood-pile—in the back entryway where they stood gleaming with a thick coating of ice. After that, we filled the fireplace, which already had a hot fire in it, to overflowing; for this was a major disaster that we knew could not be repaired for several hours. Then, hoping the highway had not iced up, I drove to the telephone exchange at Caledonia and reported our troubles. Bob Wilcox called for his truck and started out in the darkness to work on the phone line, with an admonition from me to watch out for the hot power line. The power company said it was having plenty of other troubles but would head out our way from Ironton.

There is nothing disastrous about a power failure if it doesn't last too long and the thermometer isn't down around zero; but it is inconvenient. Electricity runs our water pump, as well as the furnace, cooking range, refrigerator, and lights. But by the time I reached home, Ginnie had boomed up the fire in the little wood stove that is a "must" in the country kitchen. She had shut off the upstairs rooms to save heat, and even the downstairs bedroom. Supper was sizzling on the wood stove. The candles were lighted and the house had an unusually cheerful look about it. I piled more logs on the fireplace, mixed the toddies, and took one last look at the horses in their stalls and decided to leave them in for the night.

Supper beside the open fire is a pleasant institution under any circumstances, but especially so by candlelight, and when we saw the searchlight beams of the power company repairmen up along the road, we knew they were on the job. But the power did not come on and I drew a couple of buckets of water from the cistern and put it on to heat, so we could save whatever was in the pressure tank for drinking. After supper we quickly grew sleepy, for there was no radio and not enough light for reading. So at nine o'clock we brought down the camping bedrolls and a couple of mattresses and spread them on the living-room floor.

There was so little wind outdoors that the house held its heat remarkably well. Just the same, about every two hours during the night I would wake up and pile more logs on the fire. Up the road we could still see the lights of the repair trucks and realized that, with a widespread ice storm, there must be hundreds of men out working on the lines all across the Midwest—and we felt both grateful and sorry for them. At midnight one of the boys pulled into the yard in his car and told us our line was fixed, but that the power had now gone out somewhere down the highway. At three in the morning we could see by the powerful searchlights that they were still working. But the power did not go on and I piled in more logs.

First thing in the morning we emptied the freezing unit, carrying its contents onto an open porch where the temperature was just 22°. Breakfast was soon made on the wood stove and when I went out to feed, the day seemed not unpleasant. The cattle had to lick up their feed from a layer of ice that had formed in the feed bunks, but they prefer this to being moved into the barn. And the ground was frozen hard enough to spread their hay in the fields as usual. The animals seemed to feel especially good, in fact, galloping and butting and playing as though it were spring. The mares and Cricket nickered for their corn and hay, but after they had eaten they seemed glad to head out across the frozen fields again. Next chore was to make certain the bird feeders were well stoked with grain, for they are especially busy on such a morning, and then I took a bucket of cracked corn out and scattered it under the brush piles where our bobwhites would be apt to find it. A single day of such weather doesn't bother them too much, but more than that can be disastrous, for the birds must eat often in cold weather if they are to stay strong.

When all the chores were finished, including recharging the woodbox with a big supply of logs and stovewood, we settled down for a day beside the fire. But at just about that time—seventeen hours after it had gone off—the power came on again. The furnace started, the pump went on, the refrigerator hummed, and a half-dozen lights that had been on when the power went off lighted again.

City Cow

Late in the summer of 1914—more than forty years ago— my brothers and I had a camp on Mineral Fork, one of the small, clear streams that flow down through Washington County on the Big River-Meramec watershed in the Ozarks. We hunted squirrels, swam, fished for bass, and explored the local caves. It must have been along about Labor Day when a flash flood caught us and washed us out. We hiked the ten long miles back to civilization and every one of them was doubled by the fact that each ravine, hollow, and spring branch was running a torrent and had to be traversed to its headwaters. Finally we came out at Old Mines, where our friend George Wallace warmed and fed the bedraggled quartet, then hitched the team to the surrey and drove us home to Potosi, a dozen miles away. While we had been away a war had started in Europe, although it seemed immeasurably less important than the adventure we had just been through. Yet Grandpa Hall, who was an old soldier, shook his head and seemed to hear the rattle of sabers and muskets coming closer.

Then it was time to return to the city and school, an annual hegira of some proportions since it included eight youngsters and a cow. The latter, of course, didn't ride in the coach with the rest of us, but in a freight car; and she or one of her sisters or daughters went to the city with us each winter.

There was one difference between the rest of the youngsters in the family and me. For them, we lived in the city and summers in the country were a pleasant interlude. For me, life was concentrated in those summer months and the week ends during winter when I took the train down on Friday night to stay with Grandpa Hall in Potosi. The weekdays in winter were merely a necessary evil to be lived through.

We pastured old Jersey on the block where now stand the Chase and Park Plaza Hotels in the heart of St. Louis. The block that extends from Kingshighway to Euclid and from Lindell to Maryland was, in those days, a miniature country estate containing the Bixby mansion. The house, as I remember it, faced on Kingshighway and was built of dark red brick with castlelike turrets, a carriage driveway leading up to a porte-cochere, and appropriate landscaping. Behind the house were outbuildings: a carriage house and stable and sundry smaller structures for tools and gardeners. The remainder of the block contained ample pasturage for one Jersey cow, and the fact that she grazed there has a dim connection in my mind with the fact that Mr. Bixby had been a patient of my father's, so they had become friends.

Memories come back from those days in somewhat disconnected sequence. I am certain that people who have a copybook memory of childhood can hardly be as absorbed in their present lives and interests as we are, even though these interests are a direct result of childhood.

The snow of the past week recalls a sport that youngsters of today can hardly know. When automobiles were as scarce as hens' teeth and seldom ventured on the streets after dark, and the packed snow often lay for a week or more, we would go bobsledding. Instead of coasting downhill, some courageous father would equip his Winton with chains on all four wheels. Then a dozen children would hook a couple of bobsleds on behind and we would tour the city and the county at twenty miles an hour.

The first automobile we acquired was not new. Nevertheless, it was a remarkable machine. It was a Chalmers, cut back from the dash in the manner affected today by the most expensive foreign sports models. Two great leather straps held the hood down and a large brass tank on the running board provided fuel for the lights. It was an easy starter, not like an air-cooled job owned by a friend who had regularly to carry a large can of ether for priming the cylinders through petcocks thoughtfully provided for the purpose.

I recall teaching a young lady to drive—a very stylish young siren who wore black patent-leather pumps and white spats, a white muff of prodigious size, and as a pet had a white poodle on a white leash. Coming down Forsyth Boulevard the poodle became entangled in the gears. We dashed from the road onto the sedate campus of Washington University and mowed a fine swath through the shrubbery. I tell the story only because the statute of limitations must by now apply to the damage done. And come to think of it, the rose gardens maintained in those days down the center of Portland and Westmoreland Place made a fine substitute for a florist's shop when one needed flowers for a lady, provided one could outrun the night watchman.

Those days are gone, nor will they come again. They belong to a golden age when the world was young. Yet that age was ending even as we lived it and Grandpa Hall had a prophetic ear. In that far-off autumn of 1914 he heard the rattling of sabers and muskets; I think he knew men must always keep them by their sides if they would remain free.

Country Christmas

One custom that I feel sure will survive for as long as family farming remains part of the American scene is the country

Christmas. It is a joyful and festive occasion, almost always marked by an ingathering of the clan. For although farm families scatter more widely across our continent than they did a generation or two ago, it is easy now to travel a hundred or even a thousand miles.

In the country, happily, we are less subjected to the terrific pressures of buying and selling that have, in the city, turned this most sacred of holidays into the commercial high spot of the year. The old carols are as beautiful and appealing as ever. Yet there is no denying that they lose significance when used as a sales pitch to change the philosophy of Christian giving into one of Christmas getting.

I like to think back at this season to the rural heritage of the farm families of our nation, to see how much we have retained of the concepts of such founding fathers as Thomas Jefferson—and how much we have outgrown and abandoned. Certainly we still consider farming one of man's fundamental employments and a good and natural way of life, although we no longer look upon all other economic activity as secondary and inferior to it. I doubt that we still believe country living to be essentially good just because it is country living, nor upon life in town as necessarily bad simply because it is not the life led by our pioneering forefathers. The distance separating city and country is not nearly so great as it was even a generation ago; either kind of living can be good or bad, depending on what we make it.

Certain qualities of our rural heritage remain, however, and these seem to me all to the good. Farming can still achieve a degree of independence, both economic and political, that it is difficult to develop in the city. There is also a sense of *interdependence,* especially in a community of good family farms, a sharing and a neighborliness that are expressed in some way during almost every day of the farm year. Most of all, it seems to me that we still have a deep and abiding faith in the family farm—and the farm family—as vitally important units in the democratic way of life. By this I do not mean the old-time subsistence farm, contributing little except its excess population to the well-being of America. Such farms still exist in certain submarginal areas across the country, but by and large they are on their way out. The family farm I mean is the one that is large enough, fertile enough, and sufficiently well financed to provide year-round employment for the farm family and to furnish enough income so that it can take its rightful place in the whole economic community.

But what makes our country Christmas different—if it is different—from its celebration in city or town? First of all, for most farm families it is not quite a complete holiday. We are up early, as usual; and if there are children whose stockings are hung over the fireplace, perhaps a little earlier. As usual, we bundle up for the trip out into the cold, for there are chores to be done. We even furnish a bit of Christmas celebration for our animals: an extra block of hay and handful of grain for the cattle, some carrots for the mares along with their oats, a bow of red ribbon for Veronica, the cat, and one to tie on the collars of Mike and Tiger, the Irish setters.

After breakfast we light the fire in the living-room fireplace and enjoy an hour around the Christmas tree, a beautifully shaped red cedar from the back of the farm. Then the men, to be out from underfoot, will bundle up again and head for the barn or the fields. There are new calves to show the visitors, and an outstanding young bull, machinery that is a step ahead of last year, labor-saving gadgets in the machine shed. In a country that has not been farmed clean of all wildlife cover, we may take the dogs and guns and have a short round with the bobwhites.

In the kitchen lies one of the greatest pleasures of a country

Christmas. For breakfast the eggs came from the henhouse, milk and cream from old Betsy, honey from the beehives, and sausage from last month's butchering. Only the flour for the biscuits is not native to the farm. For Christmas dinner, much the same thing is true, although perhaps the turkey came from a neighbor who makes a specialty of them, and the cranberry sauce from far-off New England. But for the rest, freezer and pantry shelves provide bountifully. Sweet and Irish potatoes, string beans and cucumber pickles, beets and spinach and corn pudding. And from the oven, spiced pumpkin pie and mince pie baking side by side, both products of the farmwife's art. We can't go back to the old-fashioned Christmas, because time does not move that way. But perhaps it is a lot more important that we go ahead to a new kind before it is too late. Thinking about the distance from Bethlehem to Oak Ridge, I wonder whether Kriss Kringle and St. Nicholas are going to make their accustomed rounds in all the countries of Europe—and whether the spirit of Christmas actually still lives in the hearts of men. Strange animals we are—the only ones on earth with the power to influence our environment for better or worse, yet keeping up a constant attack upon that environment of such violence that our very survival often seems a matter for grave doubt.

I have been reading Albert Schweitzer, the great medical missionary and philosopher, and from him I would like to quote a thought for Christmas. "That man is truly ethical," he says, "who shatters no ice crystal as it sparkles in the sun, tears no leaf from a tree, cuts no flower—for by doing so in heedless pastime, he commits a wrong against life without being under the pressure of necessity."

Early Snow

Now winter seems to have begun in earnest, with a long succession of gray and cloudy days, occasional swirls of snow and a wind with a bite to it, morning temperatures standing at 18°, and the ground frozen hard enough until noon or after to hold up a tractor in the fields. At this season weather governs the round of the day's work, except for morning and evening care of the livestock, and plans must often be made on the spur of the moment. But as any farmer knows, there is always so much waiting to be done that this is seldom a handicap.

By the time the morning coffee boils there is generally enough daylight to make out dimly the shapes of the cattle bedded down in the barn lot and see their breath rising like smoke into the air. Then the light strengthens and I note that the first chickadees and nuthatches and titmice are coming in for their breakfast of suet, scratch feed, and peanut butter.

Well before this, however, we let Veronica in at the front

door. Just outside our bedroom window is a post that once held a bird feeder, and long before daylight the old cat comes from her bed in the granary to perch atop this post and wait for us to wake up. Mike and Tiger sleep on the side porch, which is glassed in but has a small door covered with a curtain through which they can go in and out. At the first sign of a light inside, they start knocking at the dining-room door.

About six thirty, as we are finishing breakfast, Matt arrives and we pour another cup of coffe while we make plans for the day. One of the neighbors has been over with his chain saw, felling some big trees that died during the drouth and sawing up others that blew down during last summer's cyclonic winds, so there is wood to be split and hauled in as well as poles and limbs to cut into stovewood with the tractor saw. If the weather is warm and the ground thawed, a half-dozen fencing jobs are waiting. Any warm spell that is long enough to let the ground dry out will find us making the oats ground ready. And there is always manure to haul and machinery to check and repair for the crop season that lies ahead.

Winter is the time of year that tests the livestock farmer. But for taking the beef herd through the cold weather in good shape, we have found that more than half the battle is won during the previous summer and autumn. Cattle that go into the winter thin will eat a lot of feed and come out in spring thinner still. When they start the feeding season fat and in top condition, the same amount of feed will take them through with no loss in weight whatever. Moreover, the well-fed herd produces a 100 per cent calf crop, breeds back promptly, gives plenty of milk to raise a big calf, and is generally thriftier the year round. Finally, though it takes better pasture during the grazing season and a little more hay during cold weather, there is a lot more satisfaction in handling a well-conditioned herd.

Beef cattle are remarkably hardy animals, especially when well fed. Though the feeding aisles in our big barn are open, you will seldom see a cow spending the night there. Right now we're feeding hay out on the ground in the fields and there the herd beds down at night, sometimes moving into the cedar thickets if the wind blows hard. The cows have their calves outdoors, even in midwinter. We bring them to a stall in the barn for three or four days after they are born, then turn the youngsters outdoors with their mothers, and they thrive on this treatment.

It is difficult to believe that we're rounding out our tenth year at Possum Trot. By no means has it been an easy year, what with drought and short crops and prices hovering far below production costs. Yet like farmers everywhere since the beginning of time, we are filled with great expectations for the season that lies ahead.

The rains will come again and crops will grow. The herd will increase and we'll find good buyers. The business of farming is never easy, yet it has compensations that are found in few other callings. These come in working with the land and with our animals, in seeking ways to cooperate with nature instead of subverting her, in preparing the ground, planting the seed, and harvesting the crop.

january

A New Year Begins

Now that the holidays are over and the last guest has gone, our house at Possum Trot seems strangely silent. For more than a week it overflowed with youngsters and all the excitement of Christmas, as a country house should at this season and as we hope this one will in years ahead. It is time to get back to the normal winter routine of the farm: woodcutting and cattle feeding and a last round or two of the fields with Mike and Tiger as the season ends. But there are a hundred odds and ends to be tended to before spring weather breaks.

Most of the holiday season was cloudy and unusually cold, yet this Christmas will be long remembered at Possum Trot. Mother Hall had recently celebrated her eightieth birthday, and we had decided last summer that this was an event of sufficient import to warrant a gathering of the clan such as we had not attempted for many years. The ice that covered the roads on Christmas Eve almost spoiled our plans, yet everything worked out in the end; when we lighted the living-room fire on Christmas morning and started to unwrap the gifts, there were four generations of Halls on hand for the festivities.

On the day before Christmas, Arthur and Louise and their children Linda and Pete flew in from Pittsburgh. My brother

Tom met them at the airport and they drove to the farm in an adventurous journey that consumed five hours instead of the customary two. Ralph traveled from Washington by train and set out from the city with Mother and Helen in another car. Four hours later they had progressed as far as Hillsboro. Darkness had fallen and the condition of the icy road grew worse by the moment. At last they stopped, knocked on a strange door, and asked the man who answered whether he could take in three stranded travelers on Christmas Eve. He not only could, but did, turning over to them the comfortable rooms normally occupied by two schoolteacher boarders who had gone home for the holiday.

Next morning, after a full night's sleep, they resumed their journey and reached the farm safely. My sister Margaret had arrived from Pittsburgh several days earlier, although on Christmas Eve her husband Bill called long-distance to say he could not be with us. But at nine on the morning of the great day came Ricky, Amie, and Shawn, the grandchildren, with Fred and Norma, and our party was complete. From the kitchen, where Pearl made magic with the oyster stuffing, floated aromas of turkey and mince pie. Mike and Tiger, as happens on such occasions, absorbed enough affection and petting to last them for weeks.

The whole holiday season was a delight, for our guests from Pittsburgh stayed the week, and the house was filled with comfortable confusion. From the first day, after I had shown him the ropes, young Pete took over the feeding of the animals. Each morning as I would get the coffee on the stove and stir up the orange juice to give the girls an extra half hour, Pete would don boots and jacket and head for the barns. Daisy and Ribbon soon realized Pete was the one who put their corn in the mangers and brought their hay. At the big barn, cows and calves bawled as they saw him on the way.

During the week, despite the weather, we managed a hunt or two so that Pete would have the opportunity to try out his first gun. It was good sport, though we did little damage to the farm wildlife. Ginnie and Louise and little Linda, whose present ambition is to be a star ballerina, seemed also to fill their days to overflowing. But perhaps just keeping house for three men was enough to accomplish that. The week passed far too swiftly.

The new year has brought a succession of days that, though often cold, are sunny and clear. Sunsets and sunrises have been magnificent, a condition caused by dust in the air from the long drought. This also happens when a volcanic explosion sends ashes into the upper atmosphere to drift halfway round the earth. Nor does the old adage, "Evening gray and morning red sends the traveler home to bed," hold in such times, for a crimson sunrise may be followed by a day of bluest sky.

The farm chores are easier in dry weather than when it's snowy or muddy underfoot, so that we still have not brought the cattle to the barn. They eat their hay out on the ground in the fields with surprisingly little waste. But temperatures 10° colder than normal make the feed fly. Instead of browsing, the cattle stick close to the feeding ground and must have more fuel to stoke the fires of body warmth. Some neighbors report that they have fed almost double the usual amount of feed and that cattle, forced by the drought to travel far to water or to break the ice on ponds, have lost weight.

Four baby calves arrived the last week of December, and each managed to make its entry on a mild day. This means that once they have been licked dry by their mothers and nudged to their wobbly legs for the first meal of warm milk, we have no further worry with them. One heifer, Mischief Miss, dropped her first calf, a perfectly normal baby but so tiny Matt named it Cricket. A day earlier, one of the milk cows had produced a fine bull calf. The two youngsters were put into a pen together and now both mothers take turns nursing them. Rate of growth is an inherited characteristic, yet an ample milk supply in the first months is vitally important.

Myriads of Mouths

If we were to include all the living things within the boundaries of Possum Trot and depending on it for sustenance, the number of species alone would probably run well over ten thousand, while the count of individuals would be a matter of weeks of work for a corps of zoologists. Even to list them would be a huge task, for we would have to start away down with the protozoa, which include about 20,000 species, and work our way up through all the orders of the animal kingdom. Next would come the "soil fauna," the many orders and countless species of small animals that live within the earth. Then would come the molluscs, such as snails, and the arthropods, which include crayfish, millepedes, spiders, countless kinds of insects, and other classes. In addition to these are the fishes; amphibians, such as frogs; reptiles, of which we have an assortment with our snakes and turtles; the many kinds of birds; and finally the mammals, which include, in addition to our domestic animals, all of the mice, chipmunks, rabbits, squirrels, groundhogs, possums, raccoons, skunks, muskrats, a fox or two, an occasional wolf, and now and then a traveling deer.

All of these live at Possum Trot, and some of them in almost countless numbers. For all of them the farm provides the basic wherewithal to sustain life. Some depend for food upon the plants we grow and others on the wild plants that are native here. Many of them live on decaying plant and animal matter, helping to break it down into the organic and inorganic substances that furnish food for new generations of plants and animals. All are tied up in food chains where they depend on some smaller or more numerous species for food and themselves furnish food for some other species in the next higher layer of the biotic pyramid. Fortunately, only our domestic animals, our pets, and a favored few among the wild creatures, such as the songbirds and bobwhites, depend upon our ministrations for their food supply. Yet even these take up a large part of our time throughout the entire year, and especially during the winter. It starts before daylight on these winter mornings with old Veronica and the setters. Once breakfast is over, it is time to feed the livestock. First comes a bucket of corn and manger full of hay for Daisy and Ribbon, who must be shut in their stalls before we can feed Betsy and Crip and young Junior, the bull calf. He's been down in the lower end of the lot, rubbing his head in a red claybank until his white face looks like a painted Indian's; now he comes marching in with the same solemn, head-swaying walk as Rufus, his father, of whom he is the spitting image. Broad back, deep underline, straight legs, and heavy bone; one of these days Junior will be siring better white-faced calves for the farmer who takes him into his herd.

Next we carry a bucket of warm water to the hens; then head for the big barn, where cows and calves wait expectantly, their breath sending up white clouds of steam into the air if the morning is frosty. They've spent the night out in the cedar thicket along the ridge, preferring to sleep in the open rather than in the barn. The calves are fed their ration of ground corn and protein supplement in a special "creep" at the front of the barn that the cows can't enter, and then the old girls get their ration of hay, ten pounds morning and ten pounds night. Once they have eaten, cows and calves strike out for the bottom fields, where, on mild days, they still find a bit of picking.

Over across the highway are the heifers, the pick of the crop from last spring and the preceding autumn. These, until the last few days, have needed no more than a bucket of grain, but since the bad weather we have added a bale of hay to their ration. And over east of the creek are the steers, which are still finding plenty of pasture in fields that look too brown and sere to supply much forage. But when you push aside the foxtail and ticklegrass, you find the fescue growing thriftily down close to the ground. We take a bale or two of hay to them on bad days, but so far they're more inclined to play football with it than eat it; and this winter we can't spare hay for such frivolous purposes.

When we've made this round each morning and evening, a good chunk is gone from the day and we're glad that the countless other animals on the farm, from crickets to white-tail deer, can fend for themselves. Our only service to them is to keep the fields fertile and productive, the wildlife patches planted to perennials they can eat, and the bits of stream bank and woodland undergrazed so there will be plenty of native plants to furnish their food supply.

"Nature Stuff"

"Don't you ever get tired of this nature stuff?" asked a friend the other day. One of those easy questions that doesn't lend itself to an easy answer. Yet the answer is there and has been given many times and in a multitude of ways.

As has been pointed out repeatedly during the last few years, we are creatures of the first half of the twentieth century. If our times have differed sharply from other periods in history, it is chiefly in the rate of growth of scientific knowledge. And because the point of view seemed both practical and logical, we've been educated to believe that this scientific advance must work automatically for man's good.

A few rebels believe that morals have more to do with man's good than gadgets. For America and a few other favored nations, science has produced material comfort and leisure hitherto undreamed of. Yet by far the greater part of the earth's people have shared in neither of these blessings. Our half century has been torn by wars more savage and destructive than any achieved by feudal knights or Roman legions or pre- historic cave dwellers. Men live in fear that an even greater holocaust lies just over the horizon and that we are powerless to stop it.

The world today seems divided into two great armed camps, one made up of free men and the other of slaves. Al- ready, as the misery of Asia and the moral and political in- decisions of the western world push vast populations ever closer to the slave orbit, the free men are outnumbered. The fault here lies neither with science nor the scientist, though the latter must shoulder his full responsibility toward society. Rather, it seems to me to lie in a strange state of confused moral indeci- sion on the part of free men everywhere, a sort of lapse of memory as to the value of human freedom and the means by which it must be maintained. Particularly is this true of America, the strongest of free nations, where, to quote a recent article, the American sits astraddle of the universe with a chocolate bar in one hand and a soft drink in the other, wondering where he is going next.

In such a world as this, where can man turn for some sense of tranquillity and certainty? Where can he look to find a source of spiritual direction? For some inspiration upon which to build a core of inner security? My answer is to Nature—to the unchanging verities that can be found there, to the basic rhythms of life in plant and living creature. We have separated ourselves too long from these things. We have become saturated with synthetics. Highways and sidewalks insulate our feet from the soil. Even those who work directly with the land are only dimly aware that most of our vaunted technological advances during recent decades have concerned themselves very little with basic values. They have been aimed at improving the pump rather than with maintaining the well from which our resources flow. Only in Nature can we read the laws that Nature has written, obedience to which are the price of our survival.

How then can one "get tired of this nature stuff"? Emerson had his say on the matter, along with many another. "He who knows what sweets and virtues are in the ground, the waters, the plants, the heavens, and how to come at these enchantments, is the rich and royal man."

The Sun Starts North

Now that the winter solstice is a full month gone, we can readily tell that the days are growing longer and even that the sun has started its slow northward journey along the horizon. For December twenty-first is not only the shortest day of the year, and the official beginning of winter, but is also the time when the sun reaches the southernmost point of the annual journey. Just how many degrees it will travel on that northward path from now until the summer solstice on June twenty-first is something we've never calculated except by rough measure. It suffices to know that when we stand beside the big sugar maple in the yard with the barn directly to westward, the sun sets considerably to the south of it in midwinter and somewhat to the north of it in midsummer.

The gain in afternoon daylight, which amounts to some forty minutes by the end of January, has a practical application for the farmer; while he may still do his morning chores in the dark, he can now generally finish up in the evening without turning on the lights. And in a long spell of sub-freezing weather, the chores on a livestock farm may constitute a good part of the day's work. Care of the breeding herd differs greatly from steer fattening and can hardly be streamlined to the same degree, however hard we try. There must be a "maternity ward" for cows with baby calves and those about to calve. There are generally a few youngsters in the purebred herd, born to fine old cows that we've kept to the extreme limit of their usefulness, which are given extra milk from a nurse cow. This is a dairy cow kept for the purpose, which, at least here at Possum Trot, also raises a good grade beef calf of her own while helping take care of an extra one, and sometimes even provides milk for the household.

In addition to these is generally a pen of weaning calves, another lot for the young registered bulls, and still another for old Rufus, the boss herd sire. Finally, there are the yearling steers, which are wintering in the woods pasture away from the rest of the herd but must still be fed and looked over carefully twice each day.

Mid-January seems the low point of the year. Cold weather has been with us for many weeks, so long that we forget the occasional mild spell. And still winter stretches out ahead as far as we can see. Each day that the thermometer stays below freezing puts an extra strain on the feed supply, and we begin to cast an anxious eye at the dwindling pile of bales in the big barn that last September was filled to bursting. We look at the barley and wheat, which we should be able to count on for early spring grazing, but which, because of cold and lack of moisture, may have to be torn up and sown to oats or some other crop. Not one farm plan, but several, must be made in seasons like this, if we are to prepare for every contingency; and this hardly makes for either efficiency or profitable farming.

Now and then at this season we drop in at the local auction sale, and it is sad to see the condition of some animals brought in for sale from the back-country farms. There are calves whose mothers gave no milk on last summer's drought-starved pastures and then went into winter with only fodder or poor hay for feed. Somebody buys them at a bargain price, but stands a good chance of losing the animal before grass comes. We know from long experience the difference in health, stamina, and rate of gain when cow and calf graze through the summer on fertile, well-fertilized pastures; then go into winter fat and in good shape.

This is a time of year we could do without. There are gloomy days when I have a profound sympathy for those fur-bearers which hibernate or for the birds that fly south in autumn. But then comes a snowy morning when the earth might have just been born and the chickadee sings as if it were summer, or a mild evening when the sunset paints the western sky in vivid colors and the young calves chase each other across the pasture with tails high in the air. Then I decide that, one way or another, we'll somehow "make it through to grass."

Big Farms or Small

Just now I've been watching our flock of English sparrows in the sugar maple between my study window and the barn lot.

These are not the bedraggled "chippies" of the city gutter and cornice, but clean, smart-looking birds, fat as butterballs from gleaning the grain scattered by our cattle. They are bold, aggressive, and noisy—not altogether an unmixed blessing—and when spring comes we may have to discourage them. At this season we tolerate them at the bird feeders; but when mating starts, the problem will be to keep them from appropriating all nesting sites and driving away the wrens, bluebirds, and martins. Yet how many thousand insects will each sparrow harvest in the garden next summer?

Yesterday evening, as we drove up the country road just after dark, we saw a fluttering in the headlights and stopped the car quickly. There in the road sat a small brown screech owl, somewhat blinded by the lights but otherwise not disconcerted. I wondered what hunting the little fellow finds at this season when insects have disappeared and few mice venture out into the cold. Yet we hope he visits our barn, for there the mice have been attracted in countless numbers by our baled oats hay. A dozen barn owls and screech owls would certainly help here at keeping nature in balance. Owls are historically a persecuted tribe, yet of all wild creatures in a farming country they are one of the most valuable. Few other predators are so efficient in controlling the small rodents that make a tremendous toll each year of agricultural produce.

We are burning wild-cherry wood in our fireplace this winter and visitors are prone to exclaim, "What a pity." But there were many huge old cherry trees on the farm when we came here and these, as they grow old, become very brittle and lose limbs in every storm. If it happens to be summer, when the trees are in leaf, this constitutes a real danger for the cattle. The leaves start to wilt and, as they do so, develop a high prussic-acid content. The concentration is so great that we have had a few mouthfuls kill a mature cow in a matter of minutes, long before we discovered the animal and could apply a remedy. So we had a lumberman take the good logs and cut the culls for cordwood.

Often on these cold winter days we hear the ring of the chain saw—a high, disagreeable whine—from wood-lots around the valley. Sometimes it is wood being cut for logs or for home use. Too often it is a farmer sacrificing his timber to hard times, and I wonder whether the farm will go next. The pressure to force us into a belief that family farming is doomed grows steadily. Yet it seems to me that the people who predict this would do well to consider its inevitable results. If family farming is eventually supplanted by factory farming, countless thousands of small businesses—and, indeed, small communities —are equally doomed. In such a system there would be no place for the country bank, the feed merchant, the equipment dealer, or any of the others who now supply the needs of farmers with at least fair efficiency and at a profit.

We hear a great deal about this trend toward bigger and fewer farms, and about farming as a corporate, rather than a family, enterprise. The subject is of intense interest to farmers because only about 400,000 farmers are "big," while more than 4,000,000 still operate comparatively small farms as family businesses. We small farmers do it, at least in part, because we like it this way and because our farms offer an opportunity for individualism and personal freedom. We also believe that family-sized farms pay dividends to the nation as a whole, and that we create far less than our share of the surpluses that are at the heart of the so-called farm problem. If we are really obsolescent and on the way out, we want to know about it.

This question of big versus little farms is of almost equal moment to people in cities and towns. In the heart of New York we still have a stake in farming because of the cost of food. The livelihood of many in city and town is tied up inseparably with farming. Our industries process the food from the land, use farm products as raw materials, and make machines and other goods for farmers. The city banks the farmer's money when he has any; sells him tractors, trucks, farm tools, fertilizer, building materials, and equipment. Thus the share the city has in the farmer's hardships or well-being is far more than imaginary.

There are also many in cities and towns who call themselves farmers because they own—and manage, more or less actively—farm properties. Still others have farm ownership in mind for a future date, as investment for either recreation or retirement. There is almost no big city without its Farmer's Club, no town without its businessmen who include land ownership among their interests. Like other farmers, these city ones want to know if their particular-sized farm is on the way to becoming obsolete. Some of the talk about small farms being doomed comes from very high places. Yet I find as I analyze it that not much of it comes from farmers.

Of course, it is plain as the nose on a farmer's face that for almost every kind of farming and type of land there is a point at which the farm can become too small for efficient operation or for employing the farmer and his family a sufficient number of days per year to pay a living return. There are also some very poor farmers living on farms that are too small. Both groups tend to eliminate themselves, and they are about the only instances where a case can be made against "small" farming. At the same time we can cite cases where big farms, both corporate and individual, have made outstanding successes under our enterprise system. These are most often engaged in types of farming where bigness is logical; they simply prove that big farming, as well as small farming, can succeed.

Above the minimum mentioned in the last paragraph, it is not possible to measure success on the farm in terms of size.

The determining factor is the qualities that make a successful farmer. If he has these qualities, he succeeds even when he operates a small farm from choice or necessity. There have been interesting studies made in this field, in order to try to answer the question "Who should farm?" The difficulty is, of course, that even after you have answered the question correctly, you may still not have the right people working on the land. Yet these studies corroborate what can be found in any county in America: one farmer earning a decent income and creating a good life for his family on 160 acres, a second barely getting by on 1,000 acres of similar land, and a third, who lives close at hand, ruining his land and going broke on 320 acres.

I find interesting in these studies the things that seem to have little or no influence—at least, on financial success on the farm. Among these are size of farm, number of farm magazines read, ancestral stock, school training, amount of children's help, experience other than farming. On the other hand, "cooperation of the farmwife" is listed as extremely important, while the rate of the children's progress in school seems also directly related to the farmer's success. Inheriting a farm was found, in many cases, an actual handicap; although interest in rural life, basic agricultural knowledge, and a liking for farm work were important. As might be expected, managerial and business ability stand at the very top of the list in all the surveys, although you might not expect to find physical capacity and unpaid family labor at the very bottom. One thing seems clear, at any rate. The problem is far less one of big versus small farm than of getting the right farmers established on the land.

february

Zero Weather

We grow accustomed at this season to a gray landscape and sharp wind that has a knack of searching out vulnerable spots in even the warmest clothing. Then will come a night when the clouds blow away and the thermometer drops sharply. Just before daybreak we wake to find the stars still hanging in the sky, seeming much closer to the earth than in ordinary weather. A few moments later, dawn is heralded in the east by a glow along the crest of Buford Mountain.

On such days the air is sharply clear and every feature of the countryside stands etched against its background. Fields of wheat and barley are green in the sunlight, while cedars are black on the hillsides and along the fencerows. I can't say that we like this colder weather, especially when it drops to zero. When we start out after breakfast on the round of feeding, the oil in the tractor is so stiff that the motor turns over reluctantly, sending a cloud of white smoke from the exhaust. Matt goes to the barrels to draw off a bucket or two of black-strap molasses, which we are feeding to the cows along with their hay and silage, and it will hardly flow from the barrel.

Up at the barn lot the cows lie contentedly chewing their cuds, with their breath rising like steam above their heads. Even the small calves seem not to mind the cold, but nose about in the field where we fed hay on the ground last night. One secret of keeping the herd comfortable is the deep layer of sawdust with which the barn lot is covered. Hauled in from a nearby sawmill, this absorbs moisture better than straw and stays dry and unfrozen, so that it makes ideal bedding; in spring it can then be hauled out and spread over the fields.

If it is too cold and raw to work outdoors, we have plenty of inside chores saved up. Yet it is surprising how few days come along during winter when some outdoor work cannot be accomplished. Working in the woods is a good cold-weather chore and often there is hay to haul for the bulls and weaning calves or feed to grind in the hammer mill. On mild days we work on farm machinery, build fences, catch up on odds and ends of building, or get ahead with any of the dozen other tasks that are always waiting around the farm.

Last week we had eight calves to wean. And since weaning time happened to come during the last days of the month and the last quarter of the moon, Matt said he was going to check an old country saying that had come down from his grandfather. This was to the effect that calves weaned just at this time would not bawl. But they bawled as lustily as ever.

When everything goes smoothly, we like to finish the chores shortly after five o'clock and make sure there's a big fire going in the fireplace. Then supper is planned for six, after which we really settle down to enjoy ourselves. The typewriter gets first call, oftener than not, and in winter is set up in the living room on a table beside the fire. Ginnie's darning basket, too, is handy and piled high.

But as soon as conscience will allow, these are pushed aside for reading. And this may range from *The Cattleman* and *Livestock Producer* to *The Saturday Review*, or from any of the dozen latest books on farming, gardening, and Nature

to Martin Luther's "Three Treatises," which we're reading just
now for the next session of our Great Books group in Ironton.
The dogs doze before the fire, Veronica purrs in her corner,
and long before we're ready it is time for farmers to be in bed.

Wildlife in Winter

After a fall of February snow, we can read as at no other
season the record of the wild things that manage to survive in
our bits of waste land and carry on their precarious existence
in fencerows and the shaggy cover of the hedges of multiflora
rose. Winter is no easy time for wildlife, and the various species
meet their problems in different ways. Many of the songbirds,
not being earthbound, merely avoid the issue by taking wing
for a warmer land where the sun shines bright and food is
plentiful. Yet there are others, including songbirds as well as
game birds and birds of prey, which spend the entire year with
us.

On a sunny day the little horned larks can be seen in large
flocks out on the high fields where we feed hay to the cattle.
Flashing silver in the sun, they wheel and alight to pick up
seeds that are left on the ground after the cows and calves have
eaten. Below the house along the edge of the bluff is a patch
of giant horseweed and ragweed that is a favorite place for
towhees and cardinals. These and the bluejays in the woods
above them lend color to the winter scene. Farther along the
bluff are juncos and titmice, chickadees, and the white-breasted
nuthatch with its note like a tiny tin horn. All of the woodpeckers stay with us through the winter except the redhead,
and all come to the feeders except the flicker and big pileated.
And every now and then as we hike along, we hear the cheery
voice of the Carolina wren, singing as though it were summer.

Both birds and animals must work just to stay alive during
a hard winter. Early snow beats down the cover and scatters

the seed that normally would furnish food until well into January. I suspect, however, that most of the birds except our quail have an easier time than the animals. Even the great horned owl and Cooper's hawk have an advantage, for the very lack of cover makes their hunting easier. The cottontails, fair game for every predator, still manage to survive in abundance where they are not hunted hard by man. Their tracks crisscross the yard and the barn lot in every direction, while out in the briar patches on the bluff they make regular highways through the thick cover. Yet theirs can be no life of ease and safety, for wherever they go are also the tracks of the fox. These are so numerous that many doubtless represent the doubling back of wily Reynard as he hunts across his territory. This light-footed fellow covers many a mile between dark and daylight.

A few of our mammals and also some of the cold-blooded creatures have an easier way of solving the problem of cold weather. In the ponds and along the creeks, snake and turtle and frog burrow deep into the mud to await the spring thaws. But there are also some warm-blooded mammals that hibernate for the winter; these include the groundhog, thirteen-striped ground squirrel, or gopher, and the little chipmunk. This ability to hibernate, it seems to me, is one more of Nature's wonderful ways of taking care of her children. With most mammals, including humans, the body temperature varies no more than a degree or two throughout the entire year, regardless of whether it be hot or cold. Indeed, lowering the body temperature by no more than a few degrees for any length of time results in almost certain death. The bodies of hibernating creatures readapt themselves to the condition; their temperatures may drop from a normal of 100° to no more than about 35°. If the den becomes colder than this, they awaken in time to keep from freezing. In like manner the pulse, which may normally beat at 200 to 350 per minute, sinks to only five per minute.

A winter with early snows and temperatures below normal during November and December makes a tremendous difference in the feeding and ranging habits of such species as bobwhite. Indeed, we find that we must reexamine the theory that a simple pattern of good land use such as we try to carry out at Possum Trot will inevitably pay a dividend in wildlife numbers. Already we have determined that such measures as pasture improvement, even with a tremendous step-up in soil fertility, may actually result in a decline in wildlife. For where the land is improved, it must also be used if it is to return a profit, and by autumn most fields have been harvested clean of cover and food.

We have attempted to provide this necessary food and cover by fencing out and planting small areas of waste land and setting out food patches around the ponds. So far, the plants used for this work have been multiflora rose for the fencing and the various lespedezas for food, these including Korean, bicolor, and sericea. These are either perennials or are self-seeding, but we have planted cane and millet, which are annuals, as additional food. In a normal winter these might carry the birds through. But in zero weather when the ground is covered with snow, they don't seem to do the job. Most of the seed is beaten off the plants and gets covered up, while some of it becomes watersoaked and useless long before the need for a food supply has passed.

Food is not much of a problem in farming country where many crops such as corn, soybeans, and small grains are raised, for here the birds can come out of their cover for a half hour or so and fill their crops with enough food to last perhaps forty-eight hours or more; yet such farming areas generally provide little cover. In a grassland country the birds move to the woods, where acorns, beggar's-lice, and other large seeds can supplement the food supply, or move their range entirely to the neighborhood of some far-off cornfield.

Philosophy of the Fields

With a half century coming around the bend, it is time, I think, to do a little casting up of outdoor accounts. There should be a decade, or even two, ahead to swing a gun on a fast-flying target or drop a fly into a likely looking swirl of fast water. But how does our account really stand? Have we used all those days in simply drawing out capital stock, as so many sportsmen seem to feel they have a right to do, or have any of them been spent in putting something back? And if we have made an investment, other than the purely selfish one of buying guns and tackle or supporting a shooting club, what interest have we drawn on days spent in field and woodland or along the stream? What have we seen, as we have gone along, besides the trout lying on its bed of watercress in the creel, the mallard folding in midflight to plummet into the marsh, the leap of the big buck as the bullet finds its mark?

Any lad raised in the Ozark country just after the turn of the century is almost bound to be a bass fisherman. We had more fish in those days; there is no getting around the fact. Somehow, though, it isn't the catching of fish that I remember. There was a lazy boyhood afternoon in early summer, I recall, when the fish weren't biting. I lay flat on my stomach along a high, grassy bank, gazing down into the crystal-clear water of a deep pool. And there, close to the bank, a big bass had its bed. It must have been the grandma of all the bass in that stretch of Mineral Fork and it was depositing its eggs in that circle of gravel which had been fanned clean by the male bass.

He was as big as his spouse and, once the eggs were laid, took over the entire job of watching the nest. I came back several times during the week and always the bass was there. At first he gently fanned the water with fins and tail, leaving the nest only to charge out fircely at some intruder. Soon the young had hatched, but the male bass still stayed on guard. Finally I came one day and found him gone and the nest destroyed, although it was fully a week before the period for guarding the young was over. A half hour later, wading down the stream, I saw something caught in the shallow water of the riffle. It was the big bass, all right. But he was dead and the scars of the fish gig that had killed him were plain upon his sides. Somehow, for the rest of that morning, the sun seemed to shine less brightly. Nor did the cardinals and warblers along the bank sing quite as cheerfully as usual.

Although I'll probably hunt for as long as I can carry a gun—and I started about the time I was big enough to carry one—it is not the kill that stays in memory. There have been days on the duck marsh—bright and sunny days when few birds swung in to the decoys. But on these days there were other sights and sounds to make glad the heart of an outdoorsman. Red-winged blackbirds winged across the marshland, pausing to sway on the cattails. Shore birds came—the curlew and sandpiper, the sora rail slipping through the long grasses, the plover and the killdeer and many another. And I remember one cold afternoon when the lakes were freezing fast as a blizzard swept down, and apparently a whole autumn migration passed by above us in the space of a few hours. The ducks flew at varying heights and in great bands—redheads and mallards, canvasbacks and black ducks, ringnecks, shovelers, pintails, scaups, and the rest.

Above them flew the blue geese and the great wavering wedges of Canadas whose crying could be heard above all the others. It grew colder by the minute and no birds were flying close, but still we could not leave. And finally at sunset, just as we gathered up the decoys, we heard a new sound. Far aloft we saw them—white turning to pink across the sunset sky—long lines of sandhill cranes. Such a memory is worth far more than a dozen greenheads piled alongside the blind.

The nest of the bobwhite hidden in a blackberry thicket, with its clutch of a dozen tiny eggs. The mother bird giving that soft call of alarm that freezes the young ones among the leaves until you can't see a single chick. The old bobwhite himself, sitting atop a rail fence on a bright June morning and sending his call ringing clear across the meadows. These are things I would not trade even for the picture of Mike hard down on a perfect point on opening day. Indeed, there is less and less thrill to be had from hunting any declining species, even though the hunter may justly claim that he is not the primary cause of the decline.

Although it is not popular to say so, man is no more than the most powerful of all predators that prey upon our wildlife. He is a predator when he turns the land to uses that make it impossible for the wild species to survive, just as surely as when he overshoots those species. And he is the only predator who does these things knowingly. For it is understood by all informed outdoorsmen today that the "wild" predators prey chiefly upon the surpluses over and above those which the environment can support, thus maintaining the normal balances upon which Nature insists. Too often, it is man who limits the amount of wildlife through the changes that he makes in its environment—then blames the so-called predators for the scarcity.

There is, for me, a sadness in walking through a woodland ravished by ax and fire where few of the plants and animals natural to this environment have survived. Here you will find no track of coon or possum in the snow, nor listen to the chattering of squirrels in the dawning of a June day. On the floor of such a forest, few plants grow to furnish food for turkey or deer. Even the songbirds are absent from the scene. Too often this same thing is true of our cultivated lands where fields are plowed out to the last fencerow, or pastures are overgrazed to the ultimate weed, or erosion has started the broom sedge growing on hillsides that will no longer grow a crop for man's use. Man owes a debt to Nature that he will be a long time paying.

Animals at Play

We can safely say that our calves pay little attention to the weather. On a recent day, when we had an unusually heavy rain, Matt noticed at feeding time that one of the cows had not come in. He started out to search for her and finally found her deep in the woods, a long half mile from the barn lot, with a fine heifer calf making its first attempt to stand on its wobbly legs. Matt stayed long enough to make certain the calf nursed, maintaining a respectful distance from the calf's mother since this cow has a tendency to be skittish until her calf is a week or so old. That same evening the thermometer started to drop and a biting wind came out of the northwest.

Just before bedtime, I heard several cows bawling up at the big barn and bundled up to find out what was the matter. And there, tucked well under the manger, was another new calf. It was still too young to stand, yet even in the open aisles of the barn there is protection from the wind and warmth from the feeding cattle. It dropped to 10° above zero that night, yet neither calf showed the slightest harm from the cold and it was three days before the cow in the woods even brought her calf in with the rest of the herd.

There will be a new arrival or two every few days from now on and we are hoping for mild, fairly dry weather. Actually, however, this seems to make little difference either to cow or calf. If the latter has suffered no injury in birth and manages to stand up and find its way to the dinner pail, we can be pretty sure that all is well. Once its small stomach is full of warm, rich milk, the vitality of the calf grows rapidly. For the first two or three days the cow likes to keep it hidden in some sunny spot in the woods or tall grass, where it will stay quietly for hours while she is away feeding. After that, however, it follows her on long treks across the fields, doubling the distance it travels by racing and bucking as it goes.

Playing among farm animals is not confined to youngsters, for when they're feeling in fine fettle the yearling steers and sedate old cows are as likely to join in the fun. Each evening when the herd comes up from the creek in single file, heading for the barn where their hay is in the mangers, an amusing performance takes place. There are a few fall calves with the herd and another seven heifers from our crop of last spring. These almost never head directly for the barn, but pause for perhaps a quarter hour in the pasture near the house. Here it almost seems as if they choose up sides for a butting contest, generally in pairs but sometimes as many as a half dozen, with their heads together and all pushing with might and main. After two have fought for a while, they will gallop and cavort before choosing another antagonist.

Early in the morning, when we let the mares out of the barn, they race and wheel as though to kick each other. Rufus, the bull, seems to know what's coming, for he arches his neck and blows fiercely and butts his great head against the posts of his pen. Ribbon reaches over and nips him on the back, whereupon he flicks a horn upward to fetch her a solid whack under the jaw. But the mare doesn't mind and often the performance goes on for a full ten minutes.

Daisy and Ribbon like to put on a bucking act. This, with Daisy, is mostly a matter of wheeling and rearing into the air. But Ribbon has a bit of bronc blood and bucks stiff-legged. Age seems to have little to do with this instinct for play; when we're not watching them, Tiger and Veronica play hide and seek through the house. Tiger generally goes tearing around at full clip, while the cat hides behind one piece of furniture after another, springing out to land on the dog with all four feet. And even old Mike will, on occasion, tolerate a bit of foolishness from Nuisance, the tomcat.

February is, in many ways, a season of frustration on the farm. There comes a spell of warm weather when the ground dries up and we make a start at any of a dozen tasks. The warm weather ends with rain or snow and a drop to zero, when, especially if it is windy, work outdoors must almost be abandoned. So we take on some other task in the shop or around the toolsheds and get it about halfway along when the weather warms up again. Then it's back to the outdoor job until another snow. Yet somehow the work moves forward. Fence posts are driven and wire stretched. Grass seed is broadcast on the snow so the next thaw will give it a chance to melt into the ground. And in the evenings, before the fire, we pore over the seed catalogues and decide that this season we'll try to plant no more garden than we can take care of in the few hours that are available to a farmer when summer is in full swing.

Spring Edges Closer

When the worst blizzard of winter struck the western states this week, our thermometer at Possum Trot dropped sharply and a hard wind out of the northwest rattled the shutters, sifted in through the storm sash, and set the phone wires to singing. We hurried out in the morning to have a look at the baby calves, but found them galloping about the pasture with tails high in the air as if it were summer. Then on Sunday afternoon the wind dropped to a whisper and the mercury climbed into the fifties again. After supper, when I went to make sure the biddies were safely shut up in the hen house, I heard the first spring peepers singing, down in the pond in the woods.

Little *Hyla crucifer*, smallest of all our frogs, is also the most persistent singer. Yet he could hardly be called a reliable harbinger of spring, since it is the water temperature in the ponds that seems to set him singing. There have been some years, in fact, when we have heard him tuning up in early January. This always happens when a rain has saturated the ground with water that may be considerably warmer than the air. And once he starts to sing, the little fellow will persist even when the temperature drops almost to 30°. But harbinger of spring or not, there is something optimistic about the note of the first spring peepers that braces us against the occasional spell of cold weather which may still lie ahead.

Often on these February morning the ground is frozen hard when we start out to feed the cattle, but thaws into soupy mud when the sun shines brightly during the day. When we were away for twenty-four hours last week—which is always when these things seem to happen—the cows broke into the barley field. Matt drove them out and fixed the fence, then realized he was "one cow out of pocket," to use his favorite expression. A short search located her, away off at the back water gap with a newborn calf. The weather was threatening, so Matt decided rightly that the youngster should be brought to the shelter of the barnyard. This involved carrying the calf up the steep path that climbs the bluff and is slick as glass when a thin layer of mud covers the rocks. The mother, though she is perfectly tame, grew excited and this stirred up the rest of the herd. Soon the whole sixty head were galloping behind Matt, bawling and bellowing. But he got the calf safely home.

Next day one of the steers on the east side of the farm turned up lame. Sure enough, it was Dopey, a sad sack of a fellow who seems to have a chronic foot infection that yields only to drastic treatment. This consists of the direct application of a strong carbolic solution plus a big shot of penicillin. Ordinarily we bring animals in to the pens in the barn lot, where we are equipped with a stanchion, for such treatments. But this would have meant saddling the mares and cutting Dopey out of the herd for a long trip up and back. And since he is as tame as an eight-hundred-pound steer ever gets, we decided to dose him on the spot. So Matt and I drove down with a bucket of corn, ran Dopey into a fence corner, dropped the lariat over his head, and snubbed him to a post. Then Matt reached through the fence with the nose lead and got a good grip on Dopey, losing some skin from two knuckles in the process. I gave the steer a smart slap on the rump and stuck the long needle into the leg muscle while the slap still stung, a good trick to use. In another moment I had dosed the foot, Matt released the nose lead, I unsnapped the honda of the lariat, and Dopey was on his way.

I think this was the day Ginnie planted her first garden of the year, a procedure that goes like this. She takes her basket and trowel and hikes out along the bluff through the woods to some spot that she knows from experience is especially rich in wildflowers. Here she digs up a bit of earth several inches square, being careful to disturb it as little as possible. Back at the house this is transferred into a large flat bowl, which is set in a warm and sunny spot in a south window. Here it is kept well watered, and within a few days everything starts to grow. Already I can distinguish yellow violets, wood sorrel, wild strawberry, anemone, juniper moss, and a fern or two. Soon there will be others; bluets, Johnny-jump-ups, and perhaps several more. They will mature and bloom well ahead of their outdoor cousins, bringing a touch of color and warmth to the living room.

We will be busy for the next few days broadcasting clover and grass seed on the barley, making the drill ready for oats sowing when the first dry spell comes, building fence, and bringing in the baby calves. And so the cycle of the former's year has made another complete turn. Once more spring is around the corner, and we await its coming with eagerness. Taking it altogether, we would not say that country living is easy living. Farm work is hard work and it requires knowledge and aptitudes which come only with long experience. From the standpoint of dollars earned, there is little about farming to recommend it, unless one is able to employ an almost unlimited amount of capital.

Despite all this, living on and operating a family farm can be a rich and rewarding way of life for the individual or family who can successfully adapt to it. The matter is one of weighing values and then choosing what you want. For our part, we have made our choice—and we would not trade our life at Possum Trot Farm for any other that we know.